D0521213

Information Breakthrough

How to Turn Mountains of Confusing Data into Gems of Useful Information

A Guide for Every Type of Organization

Charles J. Bodenstab

The Oasis Press
Grants Pass, Oregon

Published by The Oasis Press®/PSI Research
© 1997 by Charles J. Bodenstab

This publication is designed to provide accurate and authoritative information in regard to the subject matter covered. It is sold with the understanding that the author and publisher are not engaged in rendering legal, accounting, or other professional service. If legal advice or other expert assistance is required, the services of a competent professional person should be sought.

> — *from a declaration of principles jointly adopted by a committee of the American Bar Association and a committee of publishers.*

Editor: Karen Billipp
Interior design by Eliot House Productions
Cover illustration and design by Steven Burns

Please direct any comments, questions, or suggestions regarding this book to The Oasis Press®/PSI Research:

> Editorial Department
> 300 North Valley Drive
> Grants Pass, OR 97526
> (541) 479-9464
> (541) 476-1479 *fax*
> psi2@magick.net *email*

Library of Congress Cataloging-in-Publication Data

Bodenstab, Charles J., 1931-
    Information breakthrough : how to turn mountains of confusing data into gems of useful information / Charles J. Bodenstab.
       p.   cm.
    Includes bibliographical references and index.
    ISBN 1-55571-413-7 (pbk.)
    1. Management information systems. 2. Decision support systems.
3. Management–Information services.   I. Title.
HD30.213.B63   1997
658.4'038'011–dc21   97-39492
                                  CIP

Printed and bound in the United States of America
First Edition 10 9 8 7 6 5 4 3 2 1 0
✵ Printed on recycled paper when available

Table of Contents

Dedication

Life may be thought of as a case of juggling balls.

The key is to know which are the rubber balls and
which are the crystal balls.

This book is dedicated to the crystal balls in my life—my wife Pamela,
my four children, and their wonderful families.

Acknowledgment

I want to thank Scott Edelstein for his invaluable editing and guidance in the writing of this book. His mastery of the language and ability to quickly comprehend my concepts were enormously helpful throughout the entire process of creating this volume. Finally, it was a delight to have his company and interaction during what can be a lonely process.

Introduction

How would you like to receive business reports where the pertinent information virtually jumps off the page?

How would you like to operate in an environment where your computer automatically directs you to the areas that require attention and action?

How would you like to be spared from tons of useless detail?

All these objectives *are* possible to achieve, and achieving them would mean you were operating in an information-rich environment.

This doesn't sound like the environment in which you are currently operating, does it? That is because you—and virtually all other managers—are operating in a data-rich, but information-poor atmosphere.

Data is the raw factual measurements of events, while **information** is an enhanced version of data that imparts knowledge and direction and should trigger action.

Sadly, most businesses see very little real information.

I didn't enjoy an information-rich environment in the Fortune 500 world, or at the small company I acquired in 1983 and had to quickly turn around. In the Fortune 500 world, even at the Division General Manager level, I was overwhelmed by volumes of data, and in the small business world I was hard-pressed to get *any* data that was sound, let alone information that directed me to areas of concern.

In recent years, while consulting for numerous companies, I see the same story repeated: lots of data, but little information. The stacks of computer printouts and reports in many managers' offices tell the same compelling story, over and over.

Managers themselves are fairly vocal about the problem. They know they are being denied the information they need to run their functions properly. Moreover, they just *know* the information they need is buried in the reams of data. But they don't know how to get at it.

The single most critical factor for business success in the coming years may well be how effectively you deal with information. Those managers who are focused on the key issues and events of their businesses are going to survive and prosper. Conversely, the managers who are bogged down in reams of data are going to suffer from a host of debilitating influences. Their time will be consumed and squandered by the mechanics of dealing with the masses of data. They will fail to focus on what's important. They will pursue issues that are not significant, while ignoring others that are absolutely critical. Ultimately their organizations will suffer.

The purpose of this book is to make you a more effective manager by providing you with the tools that translate data into information, and that break the syndrome of being data rich but information poor.

This book will help you accomplish this objective by illustrating a series of highly effective cutting-edge concepts and techniques. *These new tools will change the entire way you look at data and information.*

Note, however, my point is not about simply getting data faster, or merely enhancing the way you can access data from your computer. Such approaches do not begin to address the problem. In fact, there are numerous "report writer" programs offered today with just about any modern software system. There are even systems being sold that gather an endless amount of data from within a system and allow you to create bar graphs, pie charts, and so on. These approaches, however, represent an ineffective, brute-force approach to the problem. They do not get to the heart of the dilemma, and of course they do not resolve it. In fact, in many ways they *add* to the confusion by supporting the invalid premise that more is better.

The book is also not about the latest so-called "information revolution," which to some degree is further compounding the problem. The Internet and e-mail are fast becoming part of the normal business environment. Yet even people who are aggressively using these systems complain about the indiscriminate amount of both data and information these systems flood them with on a daily basis. Getting more data faster is not the solution.

The real solution lies in transforming a great deal of unmanageable data into a small quantity of highly focused, eminently useful information. This book will show you how to accomplish this objective.

Most of the book is non-technical and deals in general concepts that will help you more effectively work with data and information. These sections contain no statistics, computer technology, or complex math. It is possible to get a great deal out of this book by simply reading these chapters.

Other chapters get into specifics, so you can actually *create* systems that will implement key ideas in the book, particularly as they relate to exception reports. In these chapters, the statistics and math appear in a gray-shaded background; if you prefer, you may skip these areas comfortably. Don't tune out the chapters and sections that deal with actual applications. They offer concrete examples you may find very informative and enlightening.

So get ready for a change in your mind-set. You are about to transform the way you think about data and information. You are about to radically change the expectations that you have regarding what information is, where to find it, and how to extract it.

Understanding the Problem

During the early stages of business growth, entrepreneurs have their fingers deep into data on a day-to-day basis. They have a total understanding of the business, and are seeing data at a detail level that relates to specific events. Dialogue with employees is therefore specific, and relates to these events.

This condition represents an almost optimal information environment, since the manager is able to mentally process all the data and draw conclusions from it directly. There is no need to rely on other people's reports, since he or she can sense trends, significant changes, and areas that are calling out for action. *The manager is instinctively changing data into information.*

As the business grows in size, however, the amount of data at the detail level also grows—and soon becomes unmanageable. Weaker managers attempt to cling to the detail, and eventually become overwhelmed by the data, which they can no longer assimilate.

Prudent managers, on the other hand, learn to deal with aggregated data. For example, they start looking at total sales by salesperson, rather than knowing how each account is doing against expectations. Or they look at indices such as days of receivables or percent of total accounts past due, rather than keep track of the payment status of individual accounts.

As these managers utilize the aggregated data, however, they become aware that something quite valuable has been lost in the process. Their dialogues with subordinates have become highly general. Important questions are being couched in aggregated terms, and the answers are coming back in aggregated form. There is a tremendous loss in specifics, since all the information has been reduced to summaries and totals.

An even more serious complication is that problem areas start to become submerged in the vast pool of data, where the favorable events conceal and offset any negative information that needs attention. *Adverse situations simply do not stand out for management action.*

Software systems are now being offered that supposedly solve this problem. However, the great majority of these products utterly fail to address the key issue. Executive screens and executive information systems are being touted as the latest breakthroughs in turning data into information. But they approach the problem from the wrong end, and thereby fail to alert managers to problem areas in a timely fashion.

Typically, these systems track a wide range of aggregated data (such as sales by salesperson or accounts receivables by region). When one of these items starts to fall below some prescribed level, the executive is alerted to the problem. Then, the designers of these systems trumpet, the user can "drill down" into the detail to explore the causes of the deterioration and take action.

Unfortunately, the software designers have missed the point. *By the time the aggregated data starts to fall below acceptable levels, many months have already passed since the problem developed.* Due to the effect of offsetting events, aggregating data actually *masks* a problem that developed much earlier at the detail level. The manager learns of a problem only after it has become serious or chronic—not when it first develops.

For example, if only aggregated data is tracked, a salesperson's performance may *appear* fairly respectable for many months after a major deterioration in performance has occurred. Although he or she may have lost several worthwhile accounts through inattention, many other accounts may continue to buy for a period of time regardless of the salesperson's performance. In addition, random events may introduce temporary sales increases that offset the lost accounts. Consequently, by the time the executive is alerted to the problem by the aggregated data and drills down to the detail, most of the damage has already occurred.

You need solutions that will alert you to such problems at the detail level *when they first develop*—while they are still easy to solve and before a major impact. For massive amounts of data this may seem like an impossible task, but as you will see, this is not only possible, but relatively simple.

Other issues that are crucial to extracting information from the data glut, include:

1. *The generation of "gee whiz" reports.* As the name implies, the recipient gets the report, and after scanning it can at best simply say, "Gee whiz!" This phenomenon stems from a misguided concept of what information is all about. The implication is that more is better; however, the opposite is true.

2. *The need to focus on action. All* reports should be action reports. A good report should virtually *demand* action on the issues it raises.

3. *The confusion of precision and accuracy.* Often reports are very precise insofar as they are carried out to a great number of decimals. The implication is that with all these decimals, the report must be extremely accurate. No way! Precision and accuracy are not the same. Sometimes one can preclude or displace the other.

4. *The overproduction of data.* Computers are information machines. Theoretically, they present us with a tremendous opportunity to generate vast amounts of information. However, managers are finding they are being overwhelmed with data in the form of voluminous printouts. Data is typically badly displayed and is not translated into information.

5. *The speed of data availability.* The speed of data availability and transmission has increased at an awesome pace. The development and widespread use of computers, and of modern communication devices such as fax and EDI, has made the speed of information delivery exceed our wildest imagination of just a decade ago. This speed of delivery has done *nothing*, however, to improve the information content of the data. It may even compound the problem by inundating the recipient.

Given this array of problems, it may seem impossible for a manager to establish and operate in a really effective information environment. While this is no small objective, the fact is it is possible to create a radically-enhanced information environment in a firm of any size. The following chapters will show you how.

The Power of Historical Perspective

To begin, let's take a fairly easy-to-understand crack at this issue of turning data into information. This will have to do with the way we display data.

The traditional technique of using "current month" and "year-to-date" is an appalling way of displaying information. This tradition had to have been started by some demented accountant from the eighteenth century who was determined to hobble business progress into future generations.

Think about this form of display for one minute. First, "year-to-date" presents a constantly changing baseline based on a constantly growing number of months as we move forward in the year. Early in the year the figures are very unstable, changing quickly for each new month added. As the year matures, the numbers become very sluggish and stable, since the addition of one month does relatively little to change the value.

Secondly, the year-to-date figure has no immediate relevance to the current month, since the one figure is for one month only and the other is for some ever-changing number of months. *If you do nothing else but change the year-to-date figure into "average month, year-to-date"* (by dividing the total year-to-date figure by the number of months), then you would turn some relatively useless data into genuine information—and the difference in the two monthly figures would become quickly apparent.

For example:

Assume you are looking at telephone expense figures for the month of May, as shown below with the traditional display for year to date:

	May	Five Months, Year-To-Date
Telephone Expense	$3,465	$14,780

Unless you have tremendous mental powers of arithmetic, there is no way you can quickly draw any clear inference from the above figures by simply glancing at the data. Is your current month of spending in this account running higher than normal? Lower than normal? It is not immediately obvious by glancing at this data display.

But, if you were to divide the year-to-date figure by five, which would reduce the figure to the average month, year-to-date, then the display would be as follows:

	May	Avg. Month, Year-To-Date
Telephone Expense	$3,465	$2,956

Note how it is now immediately apparent that the current month's expenditures are running above the pattern for the year.

This example is fairly trivial, but it demonstrates how you can change fairly obscure, hard-to-interpret data into more meaningful information by using a very simple technique.

Let's play with this example a little further. If you continue to work with year-to-date information, there is a problem since the stability of the data changes significantly each month. This problem can be solved by using a **moving average** or an **exponential average** (both of which will be discussed in greater detail later). Either method gives you an average figure for one month, which becomes the baseline against which to compare the latest month.

The main characteristic of these averages is they are always based on a constant amount of historical perspective. We now have even more useful information:

	May	Avg. of Prior Six Months	Avg. Month, Year-to-Date
Telephone Expense	$3,465	$2,546	$2,956

Now add something else of interest. It is possible to track the **normal band of variation** for any series of information over time. (The actual math for this concept is offered later.) The normal band of variation creates a baseline *range* against which you can compare actual monthly figures. You can determine not only whether a certain figure is higher or lower than the *average*, but whether it is higher or lower than *normal*. If a figure for an actual month falls outside this normal band, you are alerted that something unusual has occurred. You also know this variation is probably not random, but most likely the result of a specific cause.

The normal band of variation enables you to interpret the *degree* of any variation from the average. For example, if you know that the average monthly telephone expense is $2,546 and the expense for May was $3,465, you know the telephone costs for May were $919 above average—but you still don't know whether these costs were *unusually* high. Perhaps the phone expenses tend to vary widely from month to month; or perhaps they are always higher in the spring than in other times of the year. You still don't have quite enough information to be able to accurately interpret what the May phone expenses mean. Watch what happens as soon as you add the normal band of variation to the display of figures:

	May	Average Month	Normal Band
Telephone Expense	$3,465	$2,546	$2,129–$2,963

Now the information virtually pops off the page. Current telephone expense are *definitely* running higher than normal. Moreover, you know the conclusions you just reached are based on a prior spread of data that covers a reasonable period, and not some ever-changing baseline.

Another excellent way to turn valueless data into valuable information would be to display the actual trend for the past six months, which might look like this:

	May	April	March	February	January	December
Telephone Expense	$3,465	$2,939	$2,876	$2,678	$2,238	$2,134

This display adds a further dimension of information: it reveals there has been a steady upward movement in telephone expenses.

Displaying data as an array over time can be particularly useful—and often urgent—for business. Even a statistically unprocessed trend can tell you a great deal. In fact, information should be displayed as trends whenever possible.

A final treatment of this data could be to turn it into an **exception report,** which is an excellent way to focus attention on only the items that warrant attention. An exception report displays *only* that information which is outside the normal band of variation or indicates a significant trend, or both.

By turning your data into an exception report, you not only provide a good deal of information—you have gone so far as to direct management's attention to specific areas where action is required. What a far cry from the first presentation of "current month" and "year-to-date"! Through this simple, basic example, you can see how vast the gulf between data and important information is—and how easy it can often be to cross it.

Chapter 5 will cover the concept of exception reporting in detail, and discuss some innovative ways in which you can have your computer extract information for your consideration and action. You will also go through a wide range of other techniques—some simple, some complex—that will yield a wide variety of helpful (and even startling) information.

Summary

➤ The typical categories of "current month" and "year-to-date" are abysmal ways to display information and yield very little real information. Don't accept this all-too-common approach as a given.

➤ Displaying specific figures against the average—whether a straight moving average, an exponential average, or even the average month, year-to-date—can yield information that is clear, useful, and immediately accessible.

➤ Think in terms of exception reports. You will learn in subsequent chapters some of the mechanics of achieving this objective, but for now start creating a mind-set that looks for exceptions rather than masses of raw data.

Tracking Your Organization's Vital Signs

In later chapters you will continue to develop some statistical tools that can help you turn data into information. Additionally, you will utilize these tools to develop exception reports that are quite innovative. Before launching into these areas, you need to be introduced to another approach you can take toward handling business data and making it work for you.

Most managers rely on year-end and monthly statements to tell how well the business is doing. Monthly statements, however, cover too broad a time span for adequate control. Too much can happen from month to month. More important, an operating statement may not be sensitive enough to pick up many of the day-to-day control issues.

Instead, you need something that is going to be much more timely and sensitive to the daily ebb and flow of your business. You need something (or several things) that tracks the vital signs of your business. *Each business has its own set of unique vital signs, which can yield an enormous amount of useful, detailed, and up-to-the-minute information.*

There is a good chance you are instinctively aware of this need already, and you keep your eye on one or more vital signs throughout the month. What you may not yet do, however, is think through your business in an organized way in order to formulate and gather the data you should be monitoring regularly.

I witnessed a great example of this concept at an inner tube manufacturing company I worked with. The company had annual sales of about $30 million, and the owner had devised one of the cleverest monitoring systems I had ever seen.

The heart of any rubber-based industry is the Banbury mixer, which mixes a great variety of raw materials together to create raw rubber; the rubber is then processed further into finished goods. This is a very complex process requiring both expertise and good seat-of-the-pants judgment. In this process the operators try to use as much off-grade materials (as opposed to "virgin" materials) as possible, to keep the costs in line without compromising quality.

The owner's technique for keeping track of this entire process was to receive a daily report of the percent of virgin material versus off-grade material being used in this critical mixing process. This figure kept track of how aggressively the operators were taking advantage of the cheaper materials while still achieving good final product. Since the operators resorted to the use of more virgin materials when they had trouble with the mixing process, this figure also gave the pulse-beat of the entire operation.

By tracking this figure faithfully every day, the owner was able to keep track of the economics of the mixing operation. This system had a wonderful simple elegance to it. When the operation missed a beat, alarm bells went off immediately. (The owner had more than a dozen other figures that he also tracked on a daily or weekly basis—all with equal success.)

Eventually, the company was sold, and the new management restructured it along "modern" lines. One of the first changes was to replace the existing tracking system—a very primitive but elegant device—with a standard-cost system. But this "up-to-date" system couldn't begin to provide the same timely, sensitive information. The standard-cost data came out monthly, lacking sensitivity and timeliness, and the company soon began to flounder. It never did recover from the transition, which included other, similar blunders. It was finally broken up and sold off piecemeal.

As someone who is serious about managing your business effectively, it is essential you develop and track your own set of vital signs. With the right vital signs—and the right system for monitoring them—you can achieve the same level of control that the enterprising inner tube manufacturer did.

The remainder of this chapter will give you the tools you need to identify the right vital signs in your own organization, and set up the right system for monitoring them.

You may *already* be tracking one or more vital signs unique to your business or industry. If so, this chapter will help you identify others—or more efficiently monitor the ones you are already using.

Most managers identify (or develop) their own vital signs through experience, and through trial and error, usually over an extended period of time. You need to shorten the process, and achieve the same objective with far greater efficiency by developing a fairly rigorous but easy-to-use framework. This resulting system should provide you with clear, useful information that almost jumps off the page—and that alerts you instantly when something needs your attention.

There are four phases in identifying the unique vital signs for your company:

1. Define and isolate the critical elements of information that measure the ebb and flow of your business. (Don't tune out here by telling yourself that your business is different, or can't be measured, or whatever. Every business can be tracked in one way or another.)

2. Determine the frequency the data must be reported—either daily, weekly, or monthly. There is a best tradeoff between timeliness and excess statistical noise. (Report too frequently and the information jumps around randomly and sends out false signals. Report over too long a period and the signal comes out too late.)

3. Format the information so it jumps off the page and talks to you. Information properly formatted and displayed will clearly communicate critical trends and events; information that is poorly handled may mislead or simply be unfathomable.

4. Gather the appropriate data in the most efficient, cost-effective manner, so your system of monitoring and control is easy to administer.

What Kind of Information Should You Track?

Although some information, such as sales volume, is common to most businesses, other information is very specific to your own. Consequently, your first task is to identify what indicators best measure the ebb and flow of your particular business.

For example, in the battery and tire distributorship I ran back in the 1980s, the key elements were sales, gross margins, out-of-stock levels, cash position, and overtime hours. As long as these items were under control, we were doing fine. In contrast, a service company may be interested in hours billed, performance against quoted time, and so forth. A commercial real-estate business might be sensitive to a tally of square feet of space for which commitments to buy or rent have been received.

Here is a list of the types of information that are typically useful for each primary type of business:

Distribution	Manufacturing	Consulting
Sales	*All those for distribution, plus:*	Hours booked
Cash receipts	Direct labor hours	Travel costs
Short-term debt	Scrap levels	Product sales
Order fill levels	Material use	Project status
Overtime hours	Energy use	Gross margins

The list goes on and on. The key point is that you as owner or manager can extract those pivotal measurements that keep track of the ebb and flow of *your* particular business.

Actually, you probably already *know* which items will start to look kooky when things start to go wrong. In setting up an effective vital sign monitoring system, all you are really doing is establishing a way to gather and present this information so it tips you off before the problem gets out of control.

Incidentally, don't feel this information must always be quantitative. In a project-oriented company, it may be most important to have a system indicating how projects are progressing. An elegant little example of such a project monitoring system appears at the end of this chapter.

How Often Should You Gather and Report the Data?

The timing of your data gathering and information reporting can have a big impact on the effectiveness of the system. The more frequently information is reported, the more timely the feedback will be. Obviously, daily reporting is going to be very sensitive and will keep you up on what has happened during the previous day. Some information, like the inner tube manufacturer's percent of virgin material report, lends itself to this brief a time period.

Other data, however, bounces around too much from day to day, and will send out false signals if tracked on a daily basis. At Battery and Tire Warehouse (BTW), the company I owned in the 1980s, I tracked sales dollars and gross margin percent from our computer's invoice register every three days. Why three days? A single day was simply too sensitive: the numbers jumped around too much, and I would have reacted to aberrations rather than bona fide trends. Three-day totals smoothed out the spikes and revealed the true tempo.

In your own business, daily sales totals may be just right. In another, it may take a week or more for the information to settle down. There is no simple formula for determining the right time interval. You have to combine experimentation with common sense. Don't settle for monthly reporting when more timely feedback would give you a better check on the pulse of your business.

How to Organize the Information

How information is presented makes a world of difference in how effectively it triggers action. It's often difficult to make any sense out of a raw number, such as total sales or total hours booked. The same information presented *as a percentage or ratio* may give the data instant meaning.

At BTW we converted total sales to *sales per day*. This simple conversion made the information meaningful and enabled us to immediately compare it against our sales plan, which was also expressed in sales per day.

To illustrate this point, let's look at an actual example of the vital signs log of sales activity used at BTW, shown in Figure 3.1.

FIGURE 3.1: Vital Signs Log

Month __March__   **Sales Plan, $/Day** __45.3__

(Dollars In Thousands)

| Day | Three-Day Periods | | | Average Day | |
	Dollars	G.M. %	$/Day	G.M.%	$/Day
3/3	120.3	19.0	40.1	19.0	40.1
3/6	133.6	18.4	44.5	18.7	42.3
3/9	154.2	18.4	51.4	18.6	45.3
3/12	148.5	18.9	49.5	18.7	46.4
3/15	128.0	19.2	42.7	18.9	45.3
3/18	111.9	19.1	37.3	19.0	42.9
3/21	115.4	18.7	38.5	18.9	41.6

Note that as the month started to develop (4th column), sales looked fairly good, and month-to-date sales were actually at or above plan levels from about the end of the first week through just about the middle of the month. Things started to deteriorate thereafter, and it was clearly apparent by day 21 something needed attention. This information alerted me to the trend, and I was asking probing questions of the sales force well before the month was over.

In contrast, by waiting for end-of-month sales figures, action wouldn't have been taken until well into the next month. Then it would have been another month or more before I knew if my actions had been effective.

This is not some profound high-tech concept. This is just a simple example of a basic technique to spot sales trends as the month develops. The point is this: *by having picked the proper span of time to track, by creating a sales-per-day figure, and by tracking the information in an organized and routine manner, the report provided timely, useful information that could quickly be acted upon.*

A more exotic example of a vital sign would be tracking short-term debt position. At BTW, this indicator varied wildly throughout the month, since the company's borrowing was very sensitive to daily cash receipts, which in turn were very dependent on the day of the month. Tracking daily positions, even if expressed in various ratios, wouldn't have meant too much.

Instead the borrowing level was plotted daily on a graph, as shown in Figure 3.2, with each month superimposed over the next. After a few months, the monthly patterns started to make sense, and the current month's plot immediately indicated how we were doing against other months *during the same time of the month.* (When the graph became too cluttered, a fresh display was started, saving only the past three months.) This was a real breakthrough. An area that had been previously shrouded in fog was suddenly clear and understandable in the short-term.

In Figure 3.2, the current month started out during the first six or eight days at a level that, while high, was not out of line with levels from previous months. Consequently, if the debt during those first eight days had been viewed as a single figure with no reference points, it might not have triggered any reaction. On the plot however, it becomes clear it started out at a level that raises some concern—and, sure enough, by the twelfth of the month the debt was taking off to excessive levels.

You have to make your own determination of what will work best for your own business. Percent of hours billed may make more sense than total

FIGURE 3.2: Daily Plotting of Short-Term Debt Position

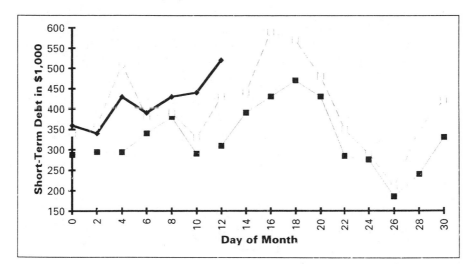

hours billed. Or overtime hours as a ratio to sales may be more significant than just total overtime hours. There are no 100 percent correct answers or absolute techniques. Whatever works best passes the test. Don't be afraid to do some experimenting.

How to Gather the Data

There is a great tendency to believe all data must come from the computer. If the data you need is readily available from the computer and easily transcribed into your vital signs log, then, of course, use it. Do *not*, however, pass up an opportunity to gather the data manually if that is the fastest way to initiate the system and get the results on a regular basis. In fact, the data you need may not be in the normal computer flow at all.

For example, you may get your sales and gross margin data from routine computer runs. Perhaps it's difficult to gather the data any other way. But you might most easily collect overtime data manually from time cards.

"Intensive Care" Monitoring

There may be times when simply monitoring the basic vital signs of a business is not sufficient, such as when a sudden major shift requires a strong and swift response. The situation is analogous to the monitoring required when a patient is in intensive care. In this situation it may be necessary to create a special one-time information-gathering and reporting system.

For example, when I was the general manager of the communications wire division at General Cable, demand exploded for a particular type of interior wire after the 1972 California earthquake. Suddenly we were under the gun to produce well beyond normal levels—and quickly! Production started to increase, but not at the rate that we desperately required. A tremendous sense of urgency needed to be created among the employees (including top managers)—and created fast.

The solution was to have each shift superintendent phone the vice-president of manufacturing—at home, if necessary—and report the production figures after each shift. While this may have violated a whole array of normal management principles—bypassing layers of management—it got attention and, more important, results. (The system was dropped as soon as the numbers began to come up strong.)

You don't want to overwork this sort of approach, but when the need exists it's a powerful addition to your regular tracking systems.

Tracking the Vital Signs of Particular Projects

The tracking of individual projects calls for a different approach. Consulting companies, design firms, real estate businesses and many other firms are very project-oriented. A monthly operating statement won't track the vital signs of such an operation or provide short-term control. In fact, for such a business it may make sense to use human judgment rather than numbers to track progress.

Years ago I was involved in an equity position with a commercial real estate firm that was almost completely project-oriented. Moreover, the projects had fairly long lead times before generating cash, which meant it was critical to track and control each project.

To stay abreast of things, the system shown in Figure 3.3 was created. Every time the rights to lease a building complex were obtained, it was added to the system, as shown in Figure 3.3 with Blackburn Hills and Southtown Plaza. Potential tenants were listed and tagged with their status as they came on the scene. The net result was a rolling display of the entire effort at two points in each month. A single glance told us what we needed to know about each complex *and* about each potential tenant. Since it was only necessary for the project leader to post a single letter of the alphabet to update an existing project (and to add any new projects that emerged during the reporting period), it was a simple task for everyone involved.

Best of all, though, a quick scan of the sheet disclosed a world of information. At a glance we were alerted to:

- ➤ Any new projects that emerged since the last report
- ➤ Any changes in status—for better or worse
- ➤ Any tendency for projects to stagnate

FIGURE 3.3: Project-Oriented Tracking

Blackburn Hills	1/5	1/20	2/5	2/20	3/5	3/20
(60,000 Sq. Ft. @ $3.00)						
Cooper Bros.	C	C	B	A	R	**
Handy Hardware	C	A	A	R	**	
Sewing Corner	C	C	B	B	B	C
Sam's Place	B	B	X			
Sing Sing	C	C	B	B	A	
Rainbow Fabrics					B	
Southtown Plaza						
(45,000 Sq. Ft. @ $2.75)						
Smart Shop	C	B	B	B	B	B
Pink Pottery	C	C	C	A	A	R
Scuba Shop	B	B	A	R	**	
The Smoke Pit	C	C	C	X		

Legend
C – Good prospect
B – Very strong prospect
A – Verbal commitment
R – Has become a receivable
** – Collected and closed
X – Bombed out

The top potential tenant, Cooper Bros., was a classic case starting out at C status (good prospect), and by February became a B or very strong prospect. In late February Cooper Bros. gave a verbal commitment, in early March it became a receivable, and soon after we finally collected and closed.

The third prospective tenant, Sewing Corner, started out in classic fashion, but by March 20 had regressed one level. Not a desirable change—but good input.

A quick look at the chart showed us the first potential tenant in the Southtown Plaza complex, Smart Shop, seemed bogged down at the B level. This initiated pertinent dialogue with the project leader: What is happening? Do you think that you might be kidding yourself? Are you being strung along? How can we generate some movement, and get Smart Shop to either commit or look elsewhere?

Within minutes after getting this project monitor twice a month, I was on top of what was going on and became alert to the tempo and pulse of the business.

Summary

➤ Every business has its own revealing vital signs that measure its day-to-day ebb and flow. There is a good chance you are tracking some of these signs in your own business already, either formally or informally.

➤ Go back over what you are doing in a more formal way to "institutionalize" the process:

- Decide exactly what information you should track. If necessary, experiment.

- Decide carefully the ideal time span each vital sign should cover—e.g., daily, weekly, twice a month, etc.

- Be innovative in how you organize and display the information. The use of simple devices such as ratios, indices, or graphs can make a big difference in how effectively the information jumps off the page.

- Think through what is the best way to gather the data—and remember, the computer is not always the answer!

➤ Remember that your entire objective is to identify, gather, and present pertinent information in such a way that it quickly grabs you by the throat when something starts to look flaky.

➤ Do something!

Some Tools to Build With

In order to go much further, you need some tools that will be essential in the process of converting data into information. In fact, these tools will be the basis for developing exception reports which, as you will see, are at the very heart of this book.

Hang in there as we explore these tools. The next chapter will merge the following concepts into a practical day-to-day system that will operate smoothly and effectively in your business environment.

Certain parts of this chapter have been shaded in gray. If you are not mathematically inclined, you can skip these sections without losing the basic concepts. On the other hand, if you are interested in learning more details about how and why certain statistical principles work, the gray-shaded sections will prove both helpful and informative.

Look at the plots of data on the following three graphs (Figures 4.1, 4.2, and 4.3). Assume this data represents sales levels for a given product for a period of 10 months. (Sales are being used as an example only; the concepts are valid for any measurement tracked over time.) Each of the three plots represents a different pattern of events. By simply eyeballing the data in each plot, you can draw fairly accurate conclusions from it.

FIGURE 4.1: Plot of Monthly Sales (Normal Pattern)

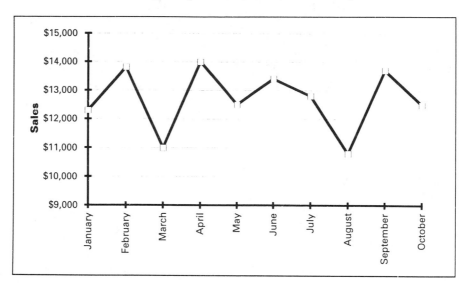

I think you would agree that the results displayed in Figure 4.1 represent a product that is moving along well within its normal band of variation. The most recent month's sales do not imply there is anything particularly significant going on. There is nothing exceptional to warrant attention. (You may not be satisfied with the *fundamental* level of sales for that item, but that is a different issue.)

FIGURE 4.2: Plot of Monthly Sales (Significant Drop)

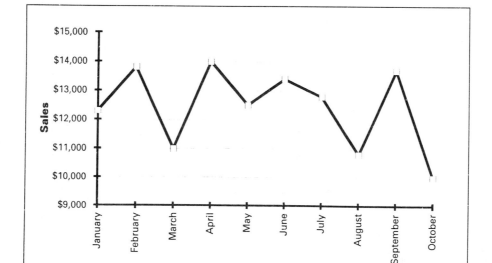

Figure 4.2 displays a different story. A quick scan of the graph intuitively triggers a reaction to the October sales level. The eye picks up the fact that something significant must have happened to drive sales outside the normal band of variation. Clearly there was some event that deserves follow-up action.

FIGURE 4.3: Plot of Monthly Sales (Significant Adverse Trend)

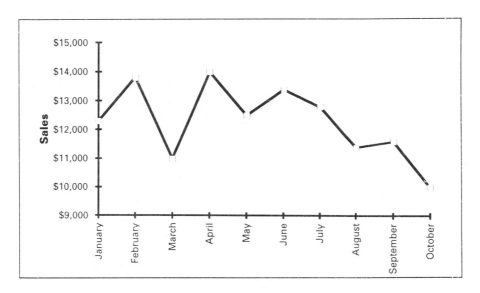

Figure 4.3 is different again. Not only is October low and outside the normal band of variation, but there is bona fide downward trend that spans a few months.

Assume you have hundreds of data series such as these for many products, organized by many locations or salespersons. The objective is to design a system that will have the computer:

1. scan all these data series,

2. ignore the ones that are like Figure 4.1, but,

3. tag and isolate the ones that are like Figure 4.2 or 4.3, and bring them to your attention.

Makes good clear sense, doesn't it?

To accomplish this objective, you will need to learn about some tools that allow you to turn data into information. These statistical devices let you track data, measure normal levels of activity, spot out-of-line events, determine trends, and so on. They are not techniques you hear about frequently, but they are very powerful devices to help you accomplish your objectives.

Ironically, these statistical techniques are not new. In fact, they were developed by European statisticians back in the 18th century. Since then these techniques have been used mainly by theoretically-oriented people who do work that is many times removed from your world and mine. I have, however, introduced some modifications to these techniques so that they work in the more practical environment that you have to deal with.

My objective is to introduce these techniques to you in such a way that you will understand how they work and easily apply them to your own business. Some of the mathematics behind these concepts are provided for those of you who want to get into the details, but the classical mathematical proofs that explain in painful detail exactly why these techniques accomplish their objectives (e.g., why two standard deviations encompass 98 percent of the points in a normal random distribution) have been dispensed with. If you can accept the fact that others have spent their lifetimes verifying these techniques, there is no need for you to dwell on these areas.

The advent of the computer has allowed these relatively old techniques to re-emerge, since the computer will do all the mathematics and provide you with the final figures and charts.

Some of these techniques have formidable-sounding titles such as **exponential average** and **mean absolute deviation**. Don't run off. You will be surprised how easy it will be to follow the concepts behind these names. As a bonus, they'll be great additions to your cocktail party vocabulary!

Establishing the Average of Something

In order to turn data into information, you will frequently want to know the *normal* or *average level* of an element of data. You will also want to constantly update the average with new information as time goes on, so that you can adjust your concept of the average to reflect recent events. This constantly-updated average will be the baseline against which you can compare and evaluate other data, and determine if there as been a significant change which warrants action.

To talk about an average, you also need another piece of terminology. Each element of data you want to process is called an **observation**. An observation can be the number of units shipped on a particular day, or the level of sales of a given item in a given month, or the height of an individual. You can take a series of observations about a common situation and use it to calculate the average value of the group of observations.

Since you are going to be dealing with business data, your observations will tend to be measurements about business events (sales, cost, output, etc.) in a given time period (a month, a week, or even a single day). This is a critical point. In a business environment, you will generally be concerned with what is known as a **time series** (e.g., a series of observations about a specific item of interest over a period of time). A classic example would be the monthly sales level for a specific customer tracked each month over a period of, say, three years.

You can arrive at an average of this type in a number of ways. One method frequently used is the classic **moving average**. In this technique you take the last four or five months of data for a particular item, then divide the total for all of the months by the number of months you used. Then, as each month passes, you recalculate the average by adding the most recent month of data and dropping the oldest. The net effect is to have an average that moves forward with time.

For example, consider these sales figures:

	Jan	Feb	Mar	Apr	May	June	July	Aug	Sept
Sales	26	25	32	33	35	28	39	43	41
5 month moving average					30	31	33	36	37

Figure 4.4 displays this same information in graph form on p. 24. Note how the moving average smooths out the actual sales, yet vividly reflects the fact that, with time, sales are gradually increasing.

The more months you use in your moving average, the more stable the average will be—but, also, the slower it will be to respond to a new fundamental shift. The reverse is true for fewer months.

FIGURE 4.4: Plot of Moving Average

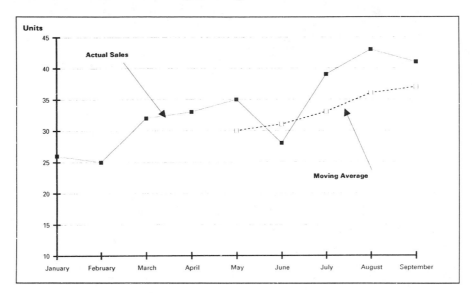

This is a fairly useful technique, as our example illustrates. A simple moving average can provide a fairly good idea of the basic level of an item being tracked. Additionally, it will smooth out the period-to-period random variations and spikes.

Building a Better Average

There is one disconcerting problem with the moving average: each month influences the average by the same amount. In other words, each month carries the same weight in determining the final average. What this means is that, with a five-month moving average, the oldest month carries the same weight as the newest month. Then, when it is six months old, it suddenly drops out of sight completely. This doesn't make too much sense, and it's certainly not the way the human mind evaluates data.

The method that I recommend for establishing a constantly-updated average is the **exponential average.** This may sound complex, but it is conceptually very simple. *The exponential average is actually nothing more than a moving average,* but with an added feature that solves the earlier problem. The exponential average has each of its elements of data *weighted* at an ever-declining rate. The weights that get applied to each observation are those of an **exponential decay curve,** such as shown in Figure 4.5.

Figure 4.5 also superimposes the weighting that occurs with a five-month moving average, so you can graphically see the difference between the two.

(Because each of the five months carries equal weight, each has a value of 1/5, or .20.)

FIGURE 4.5: Weightings

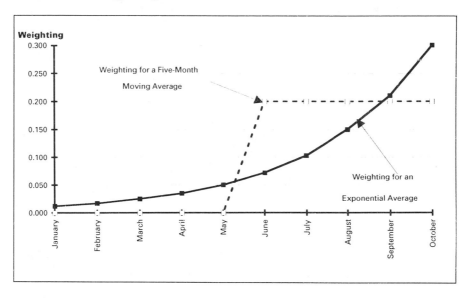

Your response at this point may be, "Wait a minute. This looks fine, but how do I get this rather complex-looking set of weightings to occur?" The actual calculations are amazingly simple, and will be pursued shortly. First a little more talk about the concept behind the weighting process.

Again, the curve shown in Figure 4.5 is called an exponential decay curve. Note the value of the curve changes where it intersects each month, from .30 in the most recent month, to .21 in the one before, to .15 in the next prior month, and then to .10, .07, .05, and so on. This illustrates the weighting each month will be given in calculating the average.

Month one (October, the most recent month) has a weight of .3, or 30%. As the average is updated with a new month of data, the new month assumes a weighting of .30, while the weighting applied to October—what had been (but is no longer) the current month—drops to .21. The same process is repeated as each month is added, so that the original month continues to have its weight reduced to .15, then to .10, and so on until its weight is hardly worth considering.

This ever-decreasing influence of an item of data is both powerful and appealing. There is a certain clear rationality to it (the more current some piece of information is, the more weight it receives), and it emulates the way we humans deal with new information.

The exponential average is one of the best techniques for expressing the current fundamental level of an item—and for tracking that item through time. As such, it is also the best method of forecasting the probable *future* level of that item.

The actual method of calculating an **exponential average** is surprisingly simple. The formula is as follows:

New average = old average × **(1.0 – alpha) + (new month data** × **alpha)**

Alpha is a pre-set constant that establishes the sensitivity of the exponential average to new data. The exponential decay curve illustrated earlier describes the weighting factors for an alpha of .30. A higher or lower alpha factor can be used to create a flatter or more curved exponential decay curve, whichever best suits the given circumstances. An alpha of .30, however, is typical, and an excellent choice for your purposes.

A key point here is that the successive application of the above calculation *automatically* causes the correct weight to be applied to each observation. There is no need to laboriously calculate a weighted average observation by observation.

To use some actual numbers:

Last month's average (or old average) = *120 units*
New month's actual sales = *140 units*
New average = *120 × (1.0 – .30) + (140 × .30)*
= *(120 × .7) + 42*
= *84 + 42*
= *126*

Notice that in an exponential decay curve, the weight applied to data never drops completely to zero. Even after many months, the system is still giving at least some trivial weight to each prior month. The key point, however, is that in contrast to the moving average, old data doesn't drop off suddenly, but gradually fades away.

Now let's address some of the practical issues that arise when we want to make use of this technique.

Initializing the Average

In order to calculate an exponential average, you have to pick an appropriate starting point. If you were to run your calculations by starting with an initial average of zero, the forecast would be constantly understated because of the influence of this first data point of zero. Conversely, if you begin with the first item of data as the starting average, it would exert an undue amount of influence until it was phased out with the passage of time.

There is a very simple solution to this problem. Take the first three or four months of data for the item in question and create a simple moving average; then use that average as the starting average. This technique very effectively stabilizes the system, and then allows future calculations to refine and update its forecasts.

The Alpha Level

The alpha level determines the shape of the decay curve (or, in other words, the rate of decay of the weighting of the data). *The higher the alpha level, the more the average will respond to new data and the faster the influence of the old data will fade out. The lower the alpha level, the slower the average will respond to new data, and the greater importance the old data will be given.*

I have found from years of experience that an alpha level of .30 is a good compromise. However, if you feel that your item to be tracked is in a state of extremely rapid change, you may consider using a higher alpha level, such as .40 (but I would not go any higher). Keep in mind, however, that this higher level will also make the system more responsive to random movements.

Measuring the Normal Range of Variation of Data

You now have an excellent technique for establishing the normal level of an item of data—its average—that will continually and automatically update itself. The next tool is a technique for measuring the normal band of variation of that item of data.

Why is it so important to know the normal band of variation? *Because your ultimate objective is to identify areas where something is happening that warrants your attention.* Therefore, by definition, we want to know when an item has gone outside of its normal range of movement. (The converse is also important. If you can identify when an item is *within* its normal band of variation, you can exclude it from consideration and attention.)

For example, let's consider the normal movement of your company's monthly sales to a specific customer. Normal month-to-month fluctuations naturally occur due to random variation. Once you have determined the range of this variation, then you know when sales for a given month fall outside of this range, something has happened that may warrant your attention.

Now look at this example in statistical terms. You can measure the normal variation of an item of data by a device known as the **mean absolute deviation, or MAD**. The mean absolute deviation is simply a measurement of the normal period-to-period variation of a particular item.

For example, if you were to look at a group of figures as shown in Figure 4.6, you could figure their average and then calculate the difference of each period from the average, as follows:

FIGURE 4.6: Determining Difference from a Fixed Average

Month	Sales	Average Monthly Sales	Difference from the Average
January	12,300	12,900	600
February	14,000	12,900	1,100
March	11,200	12,900	1,700
April	13,900	12,900	1,000
May	12,600	12,900	300
June	13,100	12,900	200
July	13,200	12,900	300
Total	90,300	(divided by 7 = an average of 12,900)	

You have been using sales figures as your example, but this concept is valid for virtually any set of data.

In computing the MAD you look at only the deviation from the average. For this purpose, *it makes no difference whether any single month's deviation is positive or negative*. In other words, if your average monthly sales total is $12,900 and in July you have stronger-than-average sales totaling $13,200, your deviation from the average is $300 (13,200 minus 12,900). In May, if sales are lower than normal, totaling only $12,600, your deviation from the average is once again 300, *not* negative 300. (All deviations from the average are expressed in positive numbers.)

The mean absolute deviation, or MAD, of all the monthly sales figures in Figure 4.6 is the average of all the differences (or deviations) from the average month. In other words, it is the average of all seven figures in the right-hand column of Figure 4.6. This is quite easy to calculate. Simply add up all the differences of the seven months in Figure 4.6 (which total 5,200); then divide this by seven, for a MAD of 742.9.

Now let's get one step more sophisticated. You can use the MAD to establish one of the most powerful tools for tracking business activity: the **normal band of variation.**

The normal band of variation is arrived at as follows: First, establish the mean absolute deviation for your set of data. Then multiply the MAD by two. (In the case of Figure 4.6, this would be 742.9 x 2, or 1,485.8.)

Next, add this number to the average monthly sales: $12,900 + $1,486 = $14,386. This gives you the upper limit of your normal band of variation.

Then *subtract* the same figure of 1,486 from the average monthly sales: $12,900 – $1,486 = $11,414. This gives you the lower limit of your normal band of variation. You have now created your full normal band of variation, which is that range of sales between $11,414 and $14,386.

Now for the pivotal point: *it is a statistical fact that, given normal fluctuations, there is a 98 percent chance that the actual sales for any given month in the future will be somewhere between these two figures.* (You would probably intuitively agree any future sales that fell outside this band would cause you to raise an eyebrow.)

Why is this concept so significant? Here's why: *when sales go outside of the normal band of variation, there is a 98 percent chance that this is because of some unusual circumstance—a circumstance that may require your attention.*

To put it another way, whenever sales go outside their normal band of variation, *pay attention*—because there is only a 2 percent chance this surge or drop in sales is due to random events. Something has changed in your organization or in the marketplace—and you'd be wise to promptly investigate what it is.

The above example is for a static situation. While this gives us a good basis to explain the fundamental concept of MAD, it does not represent a working model for implementing the concept on a routine basis. To construct a working system, I need to introduce a modification to the MAD that allows you to track data on a dynamic basis. This dynamic approach will allow you to keep updating data to reflect the constantly shifting patterns of the real world.

To proceed, use the same data as in Figure 4.6, plus data for three subsequent months. This time, however, you'll calculate an exponential average, as discussed earlier. Additionally, you will calculate the difference from that average, and then use that information to calculate the MAD. This gives us a somewhat more sophisticated view of how each month's sales stack up against expectations. Moreover, you may start to see how this is the beginning of an operating system that can be updated each month on a dynamic basis.

FIGURE 4.7: Determining Difference from an Exponential Average

Month	Sales	Exponential Average of Monthly Sales	Difference from the Average
Starting Ave.		12,500	
January	12,300	12,440	140
February	14,000	12,908	1,092
March	11,200	12,396	1,196
April	13,900	12,847	1,053
May	12,600	12,773	173
June	13,100	12,871	229
July	13,200	12,970	230
August	11,800	12,619	819
September	12,900	12,703	197
October	10,800	12,132	1,332
Total of differences from the average = 6,461			

The MAD in our example therefore is 646.1. (6,461 divided by 10–the number of observations)

Incidentally, I used the numerical average of first three months of sales as the starting average. (Using the very first month leaves it with a disproportionate influence.)

Now let's get still more elegant in your approach and track the MAD on a dynamic basis as well. You will do this by exponentially averaging the difference from the average, as shown in Figure 4.8. (These differences can be called **errors** if you think of the exponential average as a forecast of the sales for the coming month.) You will set the starting MAD as the numeric average from the first three errors.

FIGURE 4.8: Determining the Mean Average Deviation

Month	Sales	Exponential Average	Error	MAD
Starting Ave.		12,500		809
January	12,300	12,440	140	608
February	14,000	12,908	1,092	754
March	11,200	12,396	1,196	886
April	13,900	12,847	1,053	936
May	12,600	12,773	173	707
June	13,100	12,871	229	564
July	13,200	12,970	230	464
August	11,800	12,619	819	570
September	12,900	12,703	197	458
October	10,800	12,132	1,332	720

Let's go through one set of calculations to make sure you understand the technique:

The MAD for April is 936.0

The difference from the average (or the error) for May is 173

The MAD for May is therefore: (old MAD x .7) + (new error x .3)

or   *(936.0 x .7) + (173 x .3)*

                              = 655.2 + 51.9

                              = 707.1

Now let's put everything together into a graphical display that illustrates the power of the system you have just created. Figure 4.9 plots the raw sales, the exponential average, and the upper and lower band of variation that is two MADs above and below the exponential average. Note that all of these items change each month.

FIGURE 4.9: Plot of Monthly Sales and the Normal Band of Variation

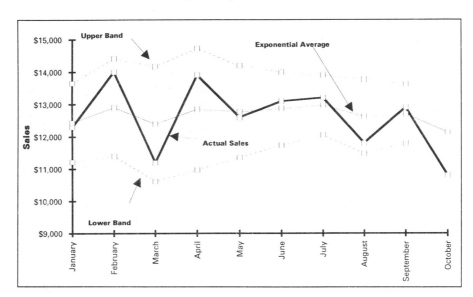

There are a number of interesting things to observe on this graph. First of all, note how the band of variation starts to narrow as sales stabilize during the May through September period. Note also how the exponential average basically stays level, smoothing out the random variations in sales.

Finally, note how October sales clearly fall outside of the band. This indicates that some event has occurred that warrants management attention.

You now have three powerful tools to help in extracting significant items that warrant management attention from a vast body of data. The **exponential average** gives you a running indication of the fundamental level of activity of an item, and the **MAD** or **mean absolute deviation** allows you to build a **normal band of variation**. If a new observation falls outside this band, there is a strong indication that something significant has impacted that item.

Equally important—if a current observation stays within the band, it means that it is experiencing its normal random movement, and little will be gained by spending time on this item. This point is critical when you are introduced to the design of specific exception reports in a subsequent chapter.

Sensing and Identifying Significant Trends

Sometimes the measure of an item will erode gradually rather than suddenly. In this case, the forces affecting the item being measured are gradual, but nevertheless persistent and significant. For example, a salesperson could be having serious personal problems that are gradually but consistently undermining performance. Consequently, there will be no single month of sales that will plunge, but there *would* be a steady downward trend.

(The focus here is primarily of downward or adverse trends, because it is these adverse patterns that require corrective action. There are also situations where an upward or positive trend merits management's attention. No problem! All the techniques covered will work equally well for trends in either direction.)

It is possible to look back over a series of points of data and perform a statistical test that informs you if the pattern represents a significant trend. This technique is deceptively simple, and operates as follows:

1. First, decide over what time period you want to test for a trend. For our example assume you want to look over the past six months of data. Specifically, you want to find out whether the last six months of sales represent a bona fide downward trend, or whether they are simply moving in a normal random pattern.

2. Check the most recent item of data to see if its value is above any of the values for one or more of the previous five months of data. Count one point for each instance in which it is above a prior month's level.

3. Test the second most recent month against the previous four months in the same way, and again count one point for every time it is higher than in a prior period.

4. Test the third most recent month against the previous three months; then test the fourth most recent month against the prior two months, and the fifth most current month against the month before.

5. Now check the total point count. If it is lower than three, then there is a 98 percent chance a significant trend exists. If it is three or above,

however, consider the item as not displaying a significant downward trend. (The test value of three for six months of data is the result of a statistical proof. Trust me, it works and is reliable.)

Three is the **test value** for a six-month period. The test values for other periods are as follows:

Number of Months Being Considered	Point Count Below Which a Trend Exists
4	1
5	2
6	3
7	5

Let's actually test out this formula on the following two groups of data that represent sales by month. (This formula will work equally well on any other measurement you decide to track.) You'll be considering the most recent six months of data throughout your examples.

FIGURE 4.10: Monthly Sales History

Month	Sales Group A	Sales Group B
January	380	398
February	400	420
March	350	380
April	310	320
May	350	410
June	360	350
July	395	330
August	320	345
September	370	310
October	330	275

Here is the same information presented graphically:

FIGURE 4.11: Monthly Sales Trends

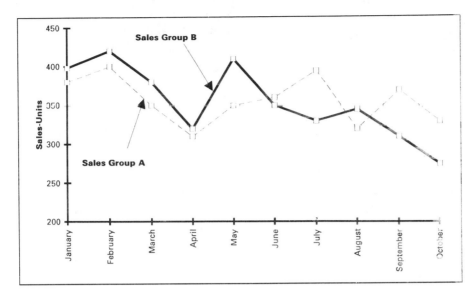

First get a point count for data group A:

October's value is above August (330 vs. 320)	*= 1 point*
September is above August, June and May	*= 3 points*
August is above none	*= 0 points*
July is above May and June	*= 2 points*
June is above May	*= 1 point*
Total	*= 7 points*

The count of seven points is higher than the test value of three, meaning the data does not pass the test, and does not demonstrate a significant downward trend. (By eyeballing the graph, you would probably confirm intuitively that the data does not really appear to have a trend either up or down.)

Now do a point count for data group B:

October's value is above no other month	*= 0 points*
September is above none	*= 0 points*
August is above July	*= 1 point*
July is above none	*= 0 points*
June is above none	*= 0 points*
Total	*= 1 point*

B's point count of one is under our test value of three—meaning that this information *does* demonstrate a significant downward trend. Eyeballing this graph gives an intuitive corroboration of this observation. Management needs to take a look at what is causing this trend.

You can use this same formula in order to find out whether a legitimate *upward* trend exists in your data. To do so, follow the same procedures described above, but in each case count a point whenever a month's value is *below*, rather than above, a previous value. A bona fide upward trend exists if your point count is less than the test value of three.

You have now added quite a few tools to your bag of tricks. Already you have learned how to quickly scan and process vast amounts of data, and focus only on the items that demonstrate a significant trend—or that have recently undergone a significant change. You are now beginning to turn reams of data into a few scant pages of highly-valuable, immediately-accessible information.

Obviously the end objective is to incorporate everything we just discussed into a computer system that performs all the functions outlined above. The chapters to come will focus on this need. The actual programming involved is virtually trivial. The biggest programming issue will be the function of gathering the appropriate time series into a logical format that will accommodate and support the techniques discussed in this chapter.

The final output format will be somewhat self-evident. You will print out only the items the system selects as having significant patterns of movement. This information should then be displayed as a time series so the pattern of the data is apparent. It is also possible (and recommended) that the data be displayed graphically. This will be quite feasible, since you are going to isolate only a small fraction of the original data. In fact, the amount isolated could be as little as three to five percent!

In future chapters specific examples of exception reporting systems for a variety of applications with illustrations of format and content will be developed.

Summary

Several tools and techniques can allow your computer to delve into a vast body of data and extract items that indicate the presence of significant events or forces that may require your attention. These tools and techniques are:

> ➤ The **exponential average,** which is simply a weighted moving average that will track the fundamental level of a given item, smoothing out the random variation.

> ➤ The **mean absolute deviation** (or **MAD),** which is a measurement of the normal random movement of an item.

> ➤ By setting a band of plus and minus two MADs around the exponential average (the **normal band of variation**), we know any new observation that falls outside of this band is due to some significant event and not due to normal random movement.

> ➤ A **trend test** will determine if a series of observations are exhibiting a significant trend as the result of an event or force that needs to be addressed by management.

The Wisdom of Exception Reports

An **exception report** is a brief, concise document that displays only the information a manager should see—information which clues in the manager that something unusual has occurred—something that requires prompt attention. The beauty of an exception report is that it pre-selects and displays only the information or items that warrant attention. Exception reports are therefore, by definition, highly focused and highly concise.

The term **exception report** has been around almost as long as the management function. "Let me see the exceptions. Don't bog me down with all this detail." This has been a plaintive cry of management for ages. Yet when is the last time you have seen an exception report? In fact, have you *ever* actually seen one?

The sad fact is, for all their usefulness, exception reports are not being produced in the vast majority of organizations—and for one very basic reason: the information management wants to see for follow-up action is by no means self-evident or obvious.

For example, assume you are a sales manager who supervises 20-some salespeople, who in turn deal with about 3,000 customers. You are currently getting the classic monthly sales reports that show sales to each customer, displayed as a total for the month, plus the year-to-date sales for each customer. This report has some value if you are interested in a specific customer (e.g., you are already familiar with the account and simply want some background prior to making a phone call). The report is virtually useless, however, in directing you to specific areas that might require your attention.

In exasperation, you ask your MIS manager for an exception report. The reply is, "What should the exceptions be based on?" After some thought, you decide you want information on those accounts that have not met their projected sales levels only.

A week or two later, your manager comes back with a new report. You look it over, and with mounting disgust say, "This is useless. Most of the projections at this point in the year don't make sense, and the exceptions make even less sense. I can't use this!"

"Well then, what *do* you want?"

"Let's see, now—give me a report that displays only those accounts where the current month is at least 10 percent under the average year-to-date month." (We are getting pretty slick now.)

After a week or two more, your manager is back with the new report. This starts looking more promising—but suddenly you say, "Wait a minute, I don't see Montoya Freight Haulers on this report, and I know there's been some concern about them."

"Oh, they were only eight percent under the past monthly average, so they didn't qualify."

"My God! For *them* to be under eight percent is critical. I would have missed them if I'd relied on this report."

By now you can see my point: the criteria you must use for information that will trigger action must usually be quite complex. Simple techniques are not going to cut it.

What you need, then, are some techniques that essentially mimic a savvy manager's thought process. Add to these techniques the power and discipline of the computer, and you can then extract information you would have isolated if you had infinite time and patience.

Granted, mimicking this thought process is a fairly tall order—but as you will recall, this is exactly what we did in the last chapter in identifying items that fell outside the normal range of variation or which exhibited a significant downward trend.

So what *can* you do in the situation described above in order to highlight items such as the eight percent drop in sales to Montoya Freight Haulers—or, for that matter, *all* the items that should command your attention?

First, you can have your computer develop exponential averages, MADs, and significant trend tests for all the historic sales data for all the accounts of your company, grouped by salesperson. Then, at the end of each month, after updating your figures, you can have the computer check to see which accounts exhibited either a significant adverse change in the last month, or a significant adverse trend over the past six months. Then you would print out *only* the accounts that demonstrated one or both of these negative changes.

Since you would be printing information on only a fraction of the accounts, you could then indulge yourself and provide added information about each account selected. For example, you could print out the monthly figures (or a graph) for the past six to 10 months, so you could actually see the pattern that triggered the problem. In fact, if you displayed this information on a computer screen, you would have the ability to probe the data bank for additional information that would further define the problem. Starts to sound interesting, doesn't it?

In structuring systems of this nature, it is amazing how effectively the basic concept works. First, there is the delight in discovering how few items are triggered for attention and how little information you have to actually examine (in contrast to the reams of reports that would normally be printed). Second, the items triggered will truly be the ones that you need to look at more closely.

Do not get me wrong, however. Not every item highlighted will always point to some startling, previously undisclosed event. For example, sales may have dropped significantly for an account, and when you look into the situation further, you discover the company's credit had been terminated due to payment problems. In this particular case this was no great insight. But the very next item highlighted could easily turn out to be the result of a major problem was just beginning to brew—and your timely warning and follow-up action may be critical in defusing something at a time when it is still responsive to a solution.

For example, after getting a sales exception report, I would query my sales-person, "Why was Baxter Marine Supply down this past month?" I'd hear back, "Oh, Charlie, those guys are totally unpredictable. You never know how much they are going to buy. Sales in any one month really don't mean anything." Then I'd show the salesperson the graph of the past eight months and point out how Baxter's recent orders are below any prior up and down movement. Now the salesperson hesitates a bit and says, "Oh, well, I think we lost their rigging battery business to Midwest Maintenance." At this point I am in a position to start asking some pointed questions. "Did we get last look? I thought we had a good relationship with them. Why wasn't our product manager involved in time to see what we could do?"

Note how this dialog is extremely timely, pertinent, and to the point—in contrast with the broad generalities that usually appear when talking about total sales.

Types of Exception Reports

Let's outline quite specifically what key elements should be considered to develop an exception report for business data. There are three conditions that qualify for management attention. They are quite distinct, and each one requires a different type of report and a different type of action.

Chronic Problems

An exception report should isolate items that demonstrate chronic or fundamental problems. These are not items that have slipped into unacceptable levels recently, but that have a chronic and long-standing nature. Your approach to these problems will differ from your approach to items that are in a state of recent or sudden change.

This is where our exponential average comes in. The exponential average smooths out the normal variations and tells us where the fundamental performance level rests.

For example, assume you are tracking monthly gross margin percentages for each of your many hundreds or thousands of customers. If you were to keep a running exponential average of the gross margin for each of these accounts, and then sort them from the poorest to the best, you could easily extract only those accounts that fell below a certain cut-off point for analysis.

An even better idea would be to isolate only the worst 50 or so performers each month, on the assumption you can deal with only so many problem areas at any one time. Then, as you straighten out items, new accounts will move up onto the list. If you are effective in your follow-up actions, the worst 50 will eventually start to look fairly decent.

You will occasionally have to add a slight modification to make a chronic problem report work in the real world. For instance, in the above example, if you produced exception reports exactly as described, you would most likely be presented with some accounts where the gross margin percent is chronically low, but where the sales levels themselves are so trivial the accounts themselves are of little interest.

A simple solution would be to have the report exclude all accounts whose average sales are below a certain dollar amount, regardless of the gross margin percentages. Now you would be seeing only the worthwhile accounts whose performance was unsatisfactory.

A further refinement to the chronic problem report is to list in the far right column the number of consecutive months the item has been on the report. This technique further highlights how long you have tolerated this item being in the bottom 50.

Incidentally, there are times when the isolation of chronic problems is *not* applicable. A case in point is the simple monthly sales report covering, say, 3,000 customers served by 12 salespeople. Significant change and trend reports will be pertinent, but unless you have a plan or objective for each account against which you can track any variance, there is nothing to measure that might indicate a chronic problem.

Significant Change

A second kind of exception report isolates items which in the most recent month (or observation) have moved outside their normal bands of variation. This is where the mean absolute deviation comes in. A report of this type alerts you to a significant event that has caused an item to move outside the band—ergo, it requires management's attention.

Do not confuse significant changes and chronic problems. The first are by definition in a state of change; the second are at a fundamentally unacceptable level. The two need to be approached with different mind-sets.

In practice, if an item starts to get in trouble, it first will appear on the significant change report. If the problem continues, it will no doubt appear again next month, and possibly on the third report. By the fourth month, however, it will have dropped off the significant change report because the continued poor performance of the item would no longer represent a significant change; but it *would* pop up on the chronic problem report, since it would by now have evolved to that state.

Significant Trend

This type of exception report highlights items that are moving in a *gradual* pattern, and therefore would not necessarily trigger your significant change criteria. Nevertheless, you want to be sure that you are looking only at items that are in a decline for a specific reason, and not just because of seasonality or chance. This where the significant trend test comes in.

Not all data lends itself to this test, however, some areas of interest simply do not have subtle movements that form trends. Either the item is O.K., or it is undergoing significant change in the specific month, or it is a chronic problem.

Combining Information from Exception Reports

There is a nice little addition that can augment our exception reporting system. If an item has triggered more than one criterion, and thus appears on more than one report during the same month or period, you can print an asterisk in the far right column by that item. For example, an item may be on the chronic problem report, but in the current month it may have experienced an even greater change than its historic pattern would justify, thereby indicating a chronic problem condition that has *significantly* worsened in the most recent month.

The applications for the exception reporting system are endless. An example, when I first took over Battery and Tire Warehouse, the company had over 3,000 accounts and 12 salespeople. The conventional sales report at the time was a monthly listing of the actual sales and gross margin percentages for each of these 3,000 accounts, sorted by salesperson. The data printed included the actual sales for the prior month, plus year-to-date sales. Each report was over two inches thick, and it was virtually impossible to see if anything significant was happening within a given salesperson's responsibility. I was reduced to monitoring each salesperson's performance by looking at his or her total sales for the month. Frequently, however, adverse events were obscured by positive events, so the total sales could look favorable even though fundamental problems were developing.

Once we started to monitor the same data with exception reports, specific, action-oriented events suddenly jumped off the page. In one case, a salesman had become an alcoholic and was drinking on the job. His sales totals were holding up fairly well, however, since he had a few very large accounts that generally bought routinely, regardless of the salesperson's performance—at least in the short run. Since the few large accounts were on a general upswing, they were obscuring the overall problem. Nevertheless, he was steadily losing smaller accounts that were sensitive to his declining performance.

It wasn't until I ran some of the first exception reports that I noticed an excessive number of his accounts popping up on the significant change reports. Ironically, it wasn't even the magnitude of the changes as much as the *number* of accounts that attracted my attention. A quick series of calls to specific accounts told the story.

Another application took place when I was with U.S. Steel. The company compiled "labor efficiency reports" that tracked the efficiency of each worker for each shift, as well as the overall efficiency of the entire plant of a few hundred employees. This report came out each week and contained a wealth of data—but the real information was obscured by the mass of detail. Again, management tended to look only at totals, which failed to pinpoint specific areas that called for attention. When the exception reports were instituted, management was immediately able to identify problems and take corrective action.

In this application all three criteria—chronic problems, significant changes, and significant trends—were applicable. The chronic problem report focused attention on the fundamentally poor performers—who, incidentally, were few in number, but had a strongly adverse impact on the plant's total performance. The significant change and trend reports focused attention on workers for whom there was a dynamic negative change due to some correctable cause (when identified early).

You now have at your disposal a variety of tools and reporting devices that can enable you to quickly, efficiently, and very effectively track the vital signs of your business. If you follow the guidance provided in this book so far, you will have on hand everything you need to stay on top of all the key functions of your organization. Furthermore, you will be routinely transforming huge amounts of data into manageable, focused, and very powerful blocks of information. In the chapters to come you'll look at some of the ways to become still more adept at keeping track of your business's vital signs.

Summary

➤ **Exception reports** are brief, concise documents that inform management something unusual has occurred—something that requires prompt attention. There are three basic types of such reports:

- **Chronic problem reports**. These isolate items that demonstrate chronic or fundamental problems. Chronic problem reports typically identify an item as chronic by using the exponential average of its performance.

- **Significant change reports.** These reports isolate items that have moved outside their normal bands of variation. Significant change is usually determined by comparing the most recent performance against a band of plus or minus two mean absolute deviations (MADs) from the exponential average.

- **Significant trend reports**. These reports call attention to any items that have started to deteriorate in a pattern that is not likely to have been caused by normal random variation.

Exception Reports
for Sales Tracking

Having discussed the concept of exception reports and the theory behind their use, it's time to describe what they would look like in an actual application.

Tracking sales activity is an excellent subject to use as the primary example, since it is an area of critical concern for just about any business. Later chapters will look at the use of exception reports in other areas such as accounts receivables, inventory tracking, and vendor performance. If any of these areas are not of interest to you, feel free to skip the chapters. However, read this chapter carefully, as it provides a vivid and concrete demonstration of how the key concepts in this book work.

Currently, your company probably tracks sales performance similar to just about every other company in existence. You get a monthly print-out of each account, sorted by salesperson, showing current month and year-to-date figures of sales dollars and gross margins. This document is about one to two inches thick, and it is impossible to use to track the movements of individual accounts.

Each month you might check out some of the larger, more important accounts, just to see how they are doing, and you might check a few accounts where you had some input indicating that a problem was brewing. But you certainly wouldn't scan every account to try to determine potential problems. Yet your past-month sales figures contain a wealth of extremely revealing information if only you knew how to extract it for ready use.

Fortunately, as a result of the tools we have designed, you *are* in a position to take this data and turn it into information. To accomplish this each month, you will create a significant change report, and a significant trend report, both of which will flag adverse situations for your attention.

You will not be creating a chronic problem report from this sales data, however, since sales figures alone do not offer a viable way to spot such problems. Low dollar sales do not necessarily correlate with a chronic sales problem at a given account. The account may simply be small, and you may even be getting the bulk of the customer's business.

The techniques you would use to create these two exception reports would be the same as the ones described in earlier chapters. Your challenge is deciding how to display the information once you have identified an account that calls for attention.

There are no absolutes regarding this issue, but Figure 6.1 represents one good approach. Figure 6.1 is a section of an exception report listing only the accounts that have been flagged for attention. The graph for Abrams & Sons, illustrates a pop-up window that a computer could display upon command for a given account. In this case it graphically displays the data for the past six months. Note how the graph validates the reason for the item being included on the exception report. (April sales are well below the normal band of variation for the prior months.)

FIGURE 6.1: Significant Change and Trend Sales Report

DSM Demo Company
April 1997

Customer Name	Nov	Dec	Jan	Feb	Mar	Apr	April of Last Year	Type of Exception
Abrams & Sons	$11,256	$16,243	$9,956	$10,265	$15,646	$4,353	$12,324	Change
Braun Hauling	$990	$1,254	$1,935	$2,341	$1,045	$123	$994	Change
Bakker Contractors	$34,287	$32,648	$47,354	$44,519	$26,398	$134	$27,689	Change
Cox Products Inc.	$55,935	$62,768	$45,111	$38,567	$31,345	$25,498	$73,459	Trend
Evenston Trucking	$5,649	$5,876	$7,869	$8,845	$7,987	$3,245	$8,456	Change
Fenton Bros.	$6,587	$3,465	$5,987	$6,756	$2,234	$3,456	$3,765	Change
Fethers Hauling	$13,254	$12,328	$11,432	$9,899	$10,999	$7,698	$16,537	Change

FIGURE 6.1: Significant Change and Trend Sales Report, continued

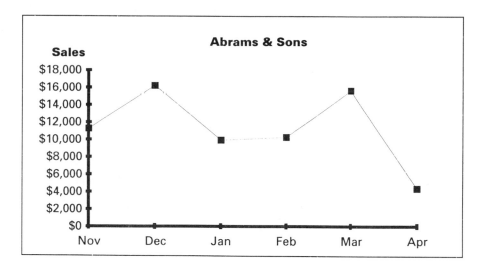

Note that the report displays the past five months in addition to the most recent month, *plus the same month from the prior year*. This display provides an immediate visual historic perspective on the data, and also allows for the comparison to the prior year, should seasonal trends exist. In addition, on the far right, this report shows why the item was triggered for the exception report—whether it was a significant change or a significant trend.

The real key to this report is that it shows *only the items that warrant your attention*. Consequently, you may be looking at only 75 accounts out of a total of 3,000, which is a vast improvement over the two-inch-thick treasury of unusable data. More important, *every single account highlighted deserves attention*. Your early intervention could prevent further deterioration, or even turn the problem around in a timely manner.

One other option: You may wish to add a low-sales override to the selection process in which the computer ignores any customer where sales are trivial—e.g., cumulative sales for the past three months are under $2,000. (Actually, the system, by its very design, tends not to highlight trivial items. Customers with minimum demand will, by definition, normally have a high variability of sales, thereby making it improbable that the current month's sales will trigger a signal of significance. For customers who buy nominal amounts, sales in any one month have no significance.)

Incidentally, you could use all the same techniques to flag customers whose purchases had *increased* in the current month beyond normal random movement. You would then be identifying situations where some positive cause and effect were occurring. (I tend not to emphasize this aspect of the concept, however, because, by and large, we are well informed about the good stuff that is taking place. It is the bad stuff that is not talked about and needs ferreting out.)

Gross Margin Tracking

Another aspect of tracking sales data relates to the gross margins of each specific account. That is, you are interested if the gross margin of an account is either suddenly deteriorating, or trending gradually and continually downward. Again, trying to extract this information from classic reporting systems is virtually impossible, unless you already have some idea what accounts to look into.

The same tools and report format could be used for this application. Figure 6.2 is a section of such a report for a specific company. The graph that accompanies the printed report is another example of a pop-up-window that reveals useful information about a particular account.

FIGURE 6.2: Significant Change and Trend Gross Margin Report

DSM Demo Company
April 1997

Customer Name	Oct	Nov	Dec	Jan	Feb	Mar	Apr	April of Last Year	Type of Exception
Alexandria Inc	19.5%	19.3%	19.6%	19.8%	19.5%	19.4%	18.1%	19.3%	Change
Cracker Postal	16.5%	17.5%	15.6%	16.0%	17.1%	15.9%	14.8%	14.9%	Change
Drew Products	20.0%	20.6%	20.6%	19.5%	20.9%	20.5%	14.9%	21.1%	Change
Higgens & Sons	19.5%	22.0%	19.7%	19.3%	19.7%	18.5%	17.9%	20.5%	Trend
Potter Printing	15.6%	16.5%	15.8%	16.0%	16.1%	15.9%	9.1%	18.9%	Change

FIGURE 6.2: **Significant Change and Trend Gross Margin Report, continued**

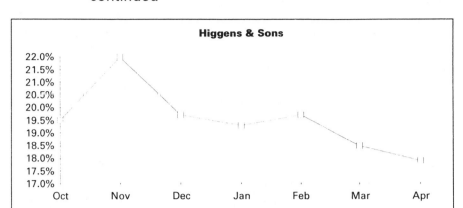

The format of the report is very similar to the one for sales tracking. Here you are looking at gross margin percentages rather than total sales dollars.

The graph is the *significant trend* for Higgens & Sons, and was brought up on command. As the graph dramatically conveys, the gross margins have been deteriorating steadily over the past five months, despite the minor upset in February. I think you would agree that this pattern of gross margin deterioration raises some interesting questions.

Incidentally, not every item selected by the system will lead to some astounding revelation. The reason for the drop could be very explainable — but at least you are now in a position to investigate the situation. In many cases the system will trigger an investigation that leads to a true revelation.

In tracking gross margins, you can add the chronic problem report, since consistently low gross margins represent an area of concern that may require action. You could therefore add a chronic problem report listing the accounts with the lowest gross margins (as calculated by their exponential average). The customers would be sorted with the worst gross margins first and the size of the report would be limited to the worst fixed number of accounts (or all those below some acceptable limit). Beware of listing *all* accounts that are below an acceptable limit. The resulting report could be fairly large, undermining our concept of action-oriented information. Since you can only take meaningful action on a limited number of accounts in any one month, it may make sense to limit the report to the worst 50 accounts and deal with those effectively. As you make progress, the worst account on the report will gradually work up to your acceptable level.

Figure 6.3 is an example of what part of this report would look like.

FIGURE 6.3: Chronic Problem Gross Margin Percent Report

DSM Demo Company
April 1997

Customer Name	Nov	Dec	Jan	Feb	Mar	Apr	Exponential Average	Months Reported
Simmons Cross	8.9%	9.1%	8.8%	9.9%	10.0%	9.4%	9.8%	9
Tracking Systems	9.9%	10.8%	10.5%	11.2%	9.8%	10.5%	10.4%	12
Small - Haskel	11.2%	11.8%	10.5%	13.0%	11.8%	12.1%	11.9%	5
Charles Gross Inc.	13.0%	12.8%	11.0%	9.0%	13.0%	11.4%	11.7%	7
Templeton Price	12.5%	12.7%	12.0%	13.5%	14.0%	12.8%	13.0%	10

An additional useful feature has been added to this chronic problem report. Note the column at the far right, "Months Reported." This is simply a count of the number of consecutive times this customer has been on this chronic problem report. This counter adds an extra dimension to the report, since it indicates the length of time this customer has been tolerated as one of the worst gross margin producers.

Sensitivity of the System

When we designed the tools to measure normal bands of variation back in Chapter 4, I mentioned that by creating a band of variation that was plus and minus two MADs on either side of the average, you would encompass 98 percent of the normal variation. The flip side to this statement is that if an observation falls outside this band, there is only a 2 percent chance it is due to normal random activity.

While I would suggest that you start with two MADs to develop your own range, there is no reason why you can't change this range to make it more or less sensitive — e.g., if the band is made wider, it will trigger fewer observations, and vice versa. Stated another way, if you find the system is triggering too many items, just broaden the band slightly; if it is triggering too few, narrow the band. The key point is to experiment until the system works best for you.

The System in Action

Once you have these exception reports available, the entire management function changes. You are now able to ask specific questions about specific situations, rather than make broad inquiries about generalities.

For instance, now you are able to go up to the appropriate salesperson and ask, "What is going on with Anderson Products? Their sales last month are down significantly from their normal levels." If you get back , "Oh, you know how they are. One month doesn't mean anything," you'd be in a position to respond, "That's simply not true in this case. Their sales for the most recent month were totally outside their normal pattern of demand." After which you might finally hear, "Well, actually, we lost their specialty item business to Baker Distribution—but I intend to get it back." You and your salesperson would then start to talk about the actual strategy for doing so, and the conversation would be truly constructive.

As you know only too well, without this kind of information and dialog, the issue would have remained a secret until it was too late for any meaningful intervention.

There is yet another benefit to these reports. Since you sorted the results by salesperson, there is an immediate awareness of the *number* of highlighted accounts for each salesperson. Even under normal circumstances every salesperson will have a few accounts appear on the report each month, for a variety of reasons. But should you suddenly see a surge in the sheer number of accounts handled by a particular person appearing on the report, this condition alone is an indication something is amiss, regardless of that person's total sales for the month.

Dealing with Seasonality

A complication arises if the sales levels of your products follow a strong seasonal pattern. With seasonality it is possible for the system we have just designed to trigger a signal that is due primarily to a normal seasonal shift, rather than a significant event requiring attention and action. In other words, it is possible for the purchases of a particular account to drop off precipitously, but only because the peak season has passed for the products this particular customer purchases. Obviously, having our exception report full of false alerts of this nature would defeat the entire concept.

It is possible to compensate for this problem by deseasonalizing the data. That is, you can manipulate the data in such a way that the seasonal effects are removed and you then apply the same techniques developed earlier, but to the processed, or deseasonalized data. The specific steps to accomplish this task would be performed by the computer and are as follows:

Ideally you will have at least two years of monthly sales for each account being tracked. (We will cover the situation of having less than two years of data later.)

Take the last 12 months of sales for each account being tracked and create a set of seasonal indices for that item for the past year. This is accomplished by adding the sales for each month to get the total for the year and then dividing each month's sales by that total, and finally multiplying the figure by 12. For example, assume that the sales for the year totaled $29,567, and the sales for July were $2,965. Then the index for July would be (2,965 ÷ 29,567) x 12 or 1.20.

Perform the same process for the preceding year's sales to establish another set of indices. You will now have two sets of indices for the two years or two indices for each specific month of the year.

Create a weighted average of the two indices, giving the most current year a 60 percent weight and the oldest year a 40 percent weight. For example, assume you calculated an index for July in the most current year as 1.20 and the index was 1.33 for that month in the previous year. The weighted average would be (1.2 x .60) + (1.33 x .40) or 1.25. The purpose of using two years weight is to smooth out aberrations between years and yet weight the most current year more heavily. You now have a single set of indices to use in your deseasonalizing process.

All that is required now is to divide the time series you are going to process by the indices for each appropriate month. The net result will be data that has had the seasonal characteristics of the specific customer's purchasing patterns removed.

Figure 6.4 displays the complete set of calculations for a specific account.

FIGURE 6.4: Deseasonalizing Monthly Data

Month	Most Current Year Sales	Most Current Year Indices	Oldest Year Sales	Oldest Year Indices	Average of Indices	Most Current Year Deseasonalized
March	$1,789	0.73	$1,555	0.69	0.71	$2,519
April	$1,987	0.81	$1,879	0.83	0.82	$2,436
May	$2,045	0.83	$1,987	0.88	0.85	$2,409
June	$2,587	1.05	$2,145	0.95	1.01	$2,565
July	$2,965	1.20	$3,005	1.33	1.25	$2,367
August	$3,568	1.45	$3,854	1.70	1.55	$2,303
September	$3,145	1.28	$2,897	1.28	1.28	$2,462
October	$2,841	1.15	$2,633	1.16	1.16	$2,456
November	$2,654	1.08	$2,222	0.98	1.04	$2,555
December	$2,212	0.90	$1,987	0.88	0.89	$2,487
January	$1,987	0.81	$1,487	0.66	0.75	$2,662
February	$1,787	0.73	$1,548	0.68	0.71	$2,522
Total Year	$29,567	12.00	$27,199	12.00	12.00	$2,463

Note incidentally, the last column of deseasonalized sales does have a relatively flat pattern compared to the two original years of sales.

If you were looking for a significant change in the above data for the new month of March you would perform all the calculations discussed earlier including the establishment of the lower band of variation as shown in figure 6.5. You would then test the new month's sales against this lower band to see if it fell below the normal band of variation. A key difference however, is you would first deseasonalize the sales for that month and test that figure against the band of variation of the deseasonalized data.

For example, assume that March sales for this account came in at $1,724, which seems low at first glance. Additionally, if you had used the raw data it would have triggered a significant adverse change signal. If you deseasonalize this element of data, however, by dividing it by its index number of .71, you get a figure of $2,428. This level is above the lower band of $2,378 and now would not trigger a reaction.

The system is saying the following about this example. While $1,724 looks relatively low compared to the sales for other months in the year, it is actually quite consistent for the month of March when you expect to see a seasonal drop in sales from this customer.

FIGURE 6.5: Processing the Deseasonalized Data

Month	Most Current Year Deseasonalized	Exponential Average	Absolute Error	MAD	Lower Band of Variation
March	$2,519	$2,481			
April	$2,437	$2,467	44	71	$2,326
May	$2,410	$2,450	58	67	$2,316
June	$2,565	$2,485	115	81	$2,322
July	$2,368	$2,450	117	92	$2,265
August	$2,303	$2,406	146	108	$2,189
September	$2,463	$2,423	57	93	$2,237
October	$2,457	$2,433	34	75	$2,283
November	$2,556	$2,470	123	89	$2,291
December	$2,487	$2,475	18	68	$2,339
January	$2,663	$2,531	187	104	$2,324
February	$2,523	$2,529	9	75	$2,378
Total Year	$2,464		82		

If you do not have a full two years of sales history for a given account, the solution is to simply work with what you have. (First of all, note you can only work with full 12 months of data. e.g., 17 months of history results is only one good year of data with which to work.)

If only one year of data is available, then perform the same calculations discussed earlier except the one year becomes the index for deseasonalizing the history. The disadvantage is we have lost the smoothing effect an additional year provides. I also suggest that items triggered for the exception report be grouped and labeled as having resulted from only one year of data so when they are viewed they will be seen as somewhat suspect.

If the account does not have even one full year of history and seasonally exists, exempt it from the process.

Summary

> ➤ The techniques developed lend themselves extremely well to monitoring sales performance.

> ➤ The two applicable reports for gaining sales performance information are significant change reports and significant trend reports.

> ➤ You can also use these same two reports to monitor gross margin percent. Chronic problem reports can be generated from gross margin data as well.

> ➤ If your products, and hence your customers, contain seasonal patterns of purchases, then add the step of deseasonalizing the data before processing it for exception reporting.

Accuracy vs. Precision

A Question of Meaning

When presenting business data or information, there is a common tendency to confuse precision and accuracy. The assumption is that if you measure something with great precision, it must therefore be very accurate. Right? Not at all!

Precision is the act of measuring something with a high level of exactness. In the business world, this process of exactness is frequently expressed by displaying data with a large number of digits. In contrast, **accuracy** is the process of expressing the true state of being of something—a genuine reflection of what is real.

In the business world, data calculated to many decimals is frequently offered up as being highly accurate. This is a fallacy, however, and a particularly dangerous one, since it implies an illusion of knowledge that is simply not valid.

The following are some situations where we can be extremely precise, but not at all accurate.

A classic case arises with forecasts or estimates. For example, the marketing department will prepare a series of sales forecasts for a variety of products. Each of these individual forecasts contains four or more significant digits (e.g., 5,678 units). All the products are then added up to create a single forecast of sales, in which the results are presented with *six* significant digits (e.g.,

59

387,981 units). This final forecast implies the last two or three digits have relevance, when in fact they do not. In 387,981 the last digit implies an accuracy of *one 10,000th of a percent*. In reality the marketing department will be very lucky if the forecast is accurate to *plus or minus five percent*.

By expressing the forecast with great precision, using six significant digits, there appears to be extreme accuracy, whereas no such accuracy exists or is possible. If the same forecast was stated as 390,000 units, it would be more sensible—and it would imply a more realistic level of accuracy.

Back in the 1950s, while I was at U.S. Steel, I worked with the company's marketing department to develop a computer model to forecast steel sales by major product category. (This represented some real early work in the area.) We met once a month to compare what our computer models were predicting with what people had come up with in conventional ways in order to understand all the factors that were critical.

In one of the meetings I noted that one of the product managers had forecasted 12,583 tons of bar stock for the next month. I said kiddingly, "John, it's interesting to note your forecast is 12,583 tons—not 12,584 or 12,582, but 12,583, right down to that last ton." He replied with a totally straight face, "Oh, actually my forecast was 13,583 tons, but my boss thought I was about a thousand tons too high."

Here is a great example of the absurd confusion of accuracy and precision. John's guess—and it *was* just an educated guess—of 12,583 tons *sounded* more accurate than 12,500, but of course it was not.

Wherever possible, make it clear you want to see information presented relative to its potential accuracy. For example, what conclusions would you draw from seeing an estimate of 387,981 units, as compared with 390,000 units, plus or minus 5 percent? The second, rounded number, offered with a range of estimated accuracy, provides more useful and realistic information than the first number with its implied (but bogus) accuracy.

Another classic situation occurs in the preparation of operating statements or budgets. Accountants calculate certain data (costs, quantities consumed, etc.) to two decimal places. Then they allocate overhead based on some highly subjective variable, such as direct labor hours, or an approximation of what each department should be charged for overhead costs. These figures may have an accuracy of plus or minus 10 percent, at best. Then, the accountants merge all the data and display the final answers—again to two decimal places. This implies an accuracy of .0001 percent. This sounds rather foolish, doesn't it? Nevertheless, this situation goes on all the time. What's more problematic is that it's easy to get drawn into the illusion.

To get a visceral sense of how we equate accuracy with precision, consider this example: Assume you are waiting for a bus, and you are told it will arrive in 30 minutes. Now, consider the same situation, except you are told it will arrive in 27 minutes. In the former case you automatically assume the time is an approximation, since it appears to be rounded to the nearest 5 or 10 minutes. In the latter situation, however, you automatically assume the time is accurate to the specific minute. (This is fine if your assumption is valid. If, however, the 27 minute projection is *also* just a rough approximation, and has been expressed to the nearest minute to create an unwarranted and illusory sense of accuracy, then you have been misled.)

This drive for more precise—and, supposedly, more accurate information—has some serious and potentially dangerous implications. As the CFO of a software company, I was badgered by the CEO to come up with profit and loss statements for each sales region. I resisted the effort, since we had some problems that were of far greater importance competing for our available resources. While we could have gathered a wide variety of data at great levels of precision (e.g., telephone costs, travel costs, salaries, etc.), our software product enjoyed gross margins of 90 percent, with a single sale grossing $200,000 to $400,000. Consequently, the highly precise regional cost information, while not immaterial from a general cost control standpoint, was pointless when commingled with the gross profit dollars.

The question of whether any region was profitable was actually very simple. Even if the region was making only one good-sized sale per month, its profitability was fantastic—and if it was not getting one sale, the month was a disaster. Commingling the precise cost figures with the gross profit figures would not have added to our ability to make intelligent decisions. In fact, it would have even *delayed* the availability of the information, since the expense data wasn't available until later in the month, while the sales numbers were available instantly at month's end.

This happens frequently among managers. Rather than dealing with an issue, there is a tendency to ask for more data or better information—when the information available is perfectly adequate to enable him or her to make an intelligent decision.

One time at Kearny National one of my subsidiary presidents indicated he was waiting for more precise data before making a decision whether or not to close a unit that was losing money. I replied, "What if the results were 10 percent better? Wouldn't the figures still indicate we should close down the unit?" The manager admitted the answer was yes, and maybe it was time to bite the bullet.

There are times when managers would be better if they used "caveman accounting": one, two, and lots. If the answer is "lots," and the same decision would be made regardless of the degree of lots, then why keep pursuing greater degrees of precision (or accuracy, for that matter)?

What are the practical implications of all this? What should you, as a manager or owner, do about it?

First, you should be simply aware of what is going on and not get drawn into the illusion. A healthy awareness of the actual degree of accuracy of any data or information is critical in the decision-making process. There is something tyrannical about figures presented with great pretensions of accuracy. These numbers imply, "I am the true word! Believe in me." You will also be a better decision-maker if you balance your use of any specific information with any other pertinent information and input at your disposal, as well as keep each item in perspective.

Finally, with this awareness you can ask questions of the people who supply you with information. These questions will challenge them to refine the entire process of information gathering and preparation.

Getting your organization to think and act differently relative to information presentation will not come automatically. Chances are you will set some people back on their heels at first with inquiries that probe the relative accuracy of the information they provide. We have all operated too long in a world that has accepted the fallacies of precision. You therefore need to help people to begin thinking along new lines. Accordingly:

- ➤ Provide some formal training and discussion of these issues. (This chapter could easily be the text for the session.)

- ➤ Give people feedback when they give you information that violates the principles of this chapter. Don't let them slip back into old habits. (They will in many cases if you let them.)

There is another aspect of confusing accuracy and precision that bears discussion here. It is an issue that gets right back to our central theme of turning data into information.

How many times have you seen accounting reports where the figures are all in the thousands of dollars, but the figures also display cents? Not only does this make the report harder to read, and the figures harder to work with, but the implied accuracy is inappropriate to the point of absurdity.

Over the past 30 years, all the comptrollers that reported to me learned early on not to submit reports that contained cents. (It was interesting to note the emotional anguish a number of them went through at the thought of dropping their cherished two decimals, which were their visual demonstration of what they thought was accuracy.) In fact, I made it clear that reports should not even contain figures with more than four significant digits, since even four digits imply an accuracy of one tenth of one percent—a level of accuracy neither of us believed. (Insistence on still fewer digits, however, may have resulted in some emotional breakdowns.)

My recommendation is that you do not allow reports to contain *any* numbers with more than four significant digits. This is desirable on two counts. First, it does not generate the illusion of inappropriate accuracy. Second, four-digit numbers are infinitely easier to read and interpret. Note the following example:

		Figures in Thousands
January	$172,234.23	$172.2
February	243,265.12	243.3
March	487,197.96	487.2
April	537,297.55	537.3
May	691,376.34	691.4
June	823,978.91	824.0

The figures to the left are the full values to the last cent. The figures to the right are the same, but displayed in thousands of dollars with one decimal. What was lost by dropping out four digits? Absolutely nothing! What was gained? Clarity and ease of comprehension.

This limit of four digits applies to the smallest numbers that will be in any array. If you have data that is a fairly even mixture of figures in the millions and figures in the hundreds of thousands, then, just for consistency, you will have to go to thousands with one decimal. If however, most of the figures are in the millions and only a few are in the hundred thousands, go to full thousands with no decimal.

Accuracy, Precision, and Planning

The use of spreadsheets to do pro-forma income and cash flow analysis is another area where the issue of precision and accuracy gets badly mauled. This is particularly true for businesses undergoing extremely rapid change and growth.

I get concerned when seeing plans that are put together for companies in just these circumstances. Typically, part of a plan deals with areas that lend themselves to fairly accurate determinations, e.g., number of analysts needed, services to be purchased, hourly rates, etc. Unfortunately, other areas have to be estimated, such as sales volume and pricing, and in these items variations of 200 to 400 hundred percent are possible. Ironically, these areas tend to have a much higher influence on the final result. In other words, if a plan is created with sales or gross margin estimates on the high side, the apparent result will be strong profitability, *regardless of the other factors and figures being used.*

Back in my U.S. Steel days, I was struck by the financial planning process for new facilities. An unbelievable amount of time was devoted to developing the anticipated capital costs for the new facility. (After all, we were an engineering and production firm, and that was what we were good at.) In contrast, the marketing people made estimates of sales and prices by the seats of their pants. Ironically, however, analysis showed that the impact on a project's profitability was profoundly dependent on sales and prices, and only marginally on the capital investment. By commingling the capital figures (which were highly detailed and precise), with the sales and pricing estimates (which were guesses), an illusion was created that the entire study was steeped in careful analysis.

There are some strong emotional and political issues at work here, of course. We all want to have the feeling that we are in control, and we tend to be emotionally sympathetic to anything that implies that we have eliminated some of the uncertainty of the real world. The trick here is to separate what is real from what may be comforting or impressive, yet at best nothing more than guesswork or a fond hope.

An old fundamental definition of business is, "Business is the process of decision making in the face of uncertainty." That uncertainty is very real, and shouldn't be masked.

On the political side, current overall business culture is enamored with quantification, computer analysis, and planning. It takes guts today to say, "The key factors that drive this proposal are not quantifiable with any degree of accuracy, so let's understand we are doing this by intuitive judgment." This is exactly what needs to be said at the appropriate time to avoid disaster.

I am not knocking planning or rigorous analytical process. Far from it. We actually have too little of it. I *am* knocking studies that allude to accuracy, when the numbers are actually a compilation of best guesses displayed with a high degree of precision.

Summary

- Develop a healthy awareness of the true accuracy inherent in any data or information you are given. Don't be seduced by the implications of accuracy implied by precise measurements.

- Recognize results are no more accurate than the least accurate component of any analysis regardless of how precisely those results are presented.

- Insist on having estimates presented as what they are, and not as if they are accurate measurements.

- Formally train your people on the concepts presented in this chapter—and provide feedback when back-sliding occurs.

- Don't spend vast amounts of time developing very precise numbers that will eventually be commingled with rough estimates—particularly when the items being estimated have a greater impact on the final results.

- Don't indulge in asking for more information as a substitute for decision making—and be sensitive to when others are doing it.

- Insist on having data and information displayed with no more than four significant digits.

Monthly Operating Statements

If there is any one area where you most need accurate, action-oriented information, it is in the monthly operating statements your accountant provides after the close of each month. These reports should tell you if you made or lost money in the prior month. Equally important, they should highlight specific areas where expenses have varied significantly from your plan, or from the prior year.

If your monthly operating statement is a crisp, clear expression of what has occurred in your company during the month—if the facts leap off the paper, signaling areas that need your attention—then you are among the small, lucky minority of business owners and managers. More often, monthly operating statements are inaccurate, badly displayed, and poorly organized. Instead of information jumping off the page, problems are hidden and obscured.

While in the Fortune 500 world, the operating reports I saw weren't anything to write home about, but it was far worse entering the small business world. Most of the monthly operating statements were virtually worthless. More alarming was the resigned attitude of the managers and owners.

I'd hear, "Yeah, you're right, the report our accounting firm churns out each month doesn't tell me a damn thing. But from what I hear from my friends in other businesses, they are in no better shape." It seemed that the only accounting report that really told them anything about profit and loss was the report for the *year end results*. For month-to-month results, they generally relied on observing cash flow or some other vital sign which evolved on its own. (See my discussion of vital signs in Chapter 3.)

A positive cash flow does not always signal fundamental profitability. It can occur because of a reduction in inventory or accounts receivables, or events that have nothing to do with operations. The result can be that cash generation looks great—even while the business is going under.

The flip side is equally bad. A temporary cash drain may obscure good results and trigger an overreaction that can ultimately hurt the business. You may see a contradiction in cash flow and true earnings so often that you tune out information that is signaling bona fide trouble.

This problem stems from the fact that accountants have failed to focus on the primary purposes of monthly operating statements: to give management information about the health of the business, and to guide them to the areas where action is needed. Instead, accountants follow a set of general procedures that are tailored more to satisfying Internal Revenue Service and Securities and Exchange Commission requirements. Hypothetically the objectives of all concerned parties should be in sync, but over the years the demands of these two agencies have seriously compromised reporting.

Most businesses have learned to live with these less-than-effective, and compromised reports. As operating margins tighten companies cannot afford to continue to fly blind.

A good operating statement should be structured so it represents the essential components of the business *as you, the operator, see it*. In order for this to happen, the breakdown of revenues and expenses has to reflect the real business as *you* know it to be—not as an accountant sees it.

The key to solving this dilemma is for you to take control. *You* have to be the person these reports must satisfy first and foremost. Only then can all the issues with the Internal Revenue and the SEC be handled—with a separate set of books, if necessary.

The operating statements at Battery and Tire Warehouse were typical. The only thing the monthly computer printout told us was the printer was working. The actual numbers meant nothing. As a result, the prior owners represented the company as making a modest profit each month, whereas in reality it was hemorrhaging.

After considerable thought and effort, I was able to redesign the monthly operating statement from the bottom up. Before long, the statement told me in no uncertain terms if the company made or lost money in the prior month. Additionally, it highlighted problem areas and displayed trends calling for action.

In another situation, I joined the board of directors for a non-profit art center in Minneapolis. The monthly operating statement was the classic accountant's report that showed current month and year-to-date—with no trends, reference points, or variances. No one knew how to read it, or really cared to. The center was also hemorrhaging financially, and came so close to closing its doors we still look back in wonder it survived and grew into the healthy organization it is today.

It took a great many actions to turn around this organization, one of which was to create a monthly operating report that enabled *everyone*—from the executive director to each board member—to read it with complete comprehension. Trends were displayed that put expenses into respective. Variances against both our plans and the prior year were clearly stated. It was immediately clear just how well the center had done in the prior month and how the year was shaping up. Soon the executive director was addressing the board about our financial performance and talking intelligently about variances, trends, and the causes behind them.

Take a look at some of the specific areas where you can make improvements in your own operating statement.

Format

One of the key areas that can make a difference is the format. Obviously, current month followed by month-to-date isn't going to do much toward changing data into information. At a minimum you will want to display trends and highlight any variances from plan and from the prior year.

For starters all operating reports for use by managers should display for the past six months, and preferably as many as 13 months of data. This way, at a minimum, you can see trends.

In addition, there should be a comparison of the current month against plan, and against the same month from the prior year. Finally, there should be a display of the year-to-date figures against the plan, and against the prior year as well.

An example of this format appears in Figure 8.1:

FIGURE 8.1: Suggested Operating Statement Layout

DSM Demo Company
Monthly Operating Statement
April 1997

Expenses	Oct	Nov	Dec	Jan	Feb	March	April	Last Yr. April	Average Month YTD
Accounting	$134	$243	$234	$546	$143	$231	$145	$ 98	$361
Bank Charges	$ 0	$ 45	$ 89	$ 54	$ 0	$123	$ 99	$ 87	$ 69
Telephones	$ 657	$769	$698	$712	$687	$786	$987	$892	$793

DSM Demo Company
Monthly Operating Statement
April 1997

Expenses	Month of April						Year-to Date				
	Cur. Month	Last Year	Plan	Variance to Plan	Year		YTD	Cur. Year	Last Plan	Variance to Plan	Year
Accounting	$145	$ 98	$ 75	($70)	($ 47)		$1,836	$1548	$1698	($136)	($288)
Bank Charges	$ 99	$ 87	$102	$ 3	($ 15)		$ 276	$ 259	$ 296	$ 29	($17)
Telephones	$ 987	$897	$769	($218)	($ 90)		$ 3172	$2958	$3001	($171)	($214)

One factor to note in these examples are all *adverse* variances are in parentheses. In preparing your own operating statement the computer should place any increase in costs as well as any drop in sales, revenue, or profits in parentheses.

Accountants seem to rebel at this convention at first, because it is, in their words, "mathematically inconsistent." Look at what is gained, however. When you scan down the column of variances, there is no question what to look for. Parentheses are bad, and big numbers in parentheses are worse. There is no need to check back to the account definitions to see if you are looking at a sales, profit, or cost variance to determine what should command your attention. The net effect is consistent with your primary objective to make the numbers jump off the page.

Breakdown of Accounts

This is the area where you may get into the greatest controversy with accountants. Nevertheless, be firm and hold your ground. You want data on salaries, medical expenses, rent, utilities, and so on to reflect your bona fide operations *and nothing else*. Make sure *you* believe these accounts reflect reality; do not accept anything else, even it outside influences call for them. Remember, your controller can always recast the data into another statement to keep the auditors and tax people happy.

The same is true of the way your accounts are arranged and sub-totaled. I was once a principal of a company that was in a rapid state of growth. Cost control was therefore utterly critical. The operating statement, as dictated by our auditors, was arranged so the cost of goods sold was accumulated in a certain way, leading to a gross margin. Their version of operating expenses followed. These were then subtracted from the gross profit to eventually arrive at a net profit. The only problem was I couldn't tell what the monthly fixed costs were, and what the "nut" was that we had to meet each month.

Finally, in exasperation, I took all the truly variable costs (e.g., those that went up or down if more or less product was sold) and, over the accountants' objections, accumulated them under one total, striking a gross margin at this point, followed by what were the true fixed expenses, which then led to the net profit. With this format there was no question about where we stood (which incidentally was not too appealing).

I also sprinkled a series of subtotals throughout the report that summarized areas such as "total salaries and fringe" and "total outside contracted services." The effect was a report whose format did not resemble anything you would see from accountants—but it gave me exactly the direction I needed.

Accruals

Accruals are a simple system of artificially charging yourself in one period when you know it is a more realistic reflection of how your business actually runs. Then, having accrued the charge, you reverse it in a later period, when the charge actually arrives. The same thing can apply in reverse—you delay a charge until the more appropriate period.

Use of accruals is a time-honored concept in accounting. Unfortunately, accruals are generally used to satisfy the accountant's view of the world—

when, instead, they should be used to clarify the reporting of operating results that satisfy the manager.

A good example of this situation existed at Battery and Tire Warehouse. There were considerable outlays for promotional material each month, which usually were offset by reimbursements from vendors. The problem was that the promotional materials were purchased in one month and the reimbursement wasn't until two or more months later. This situation resulted in major increases in expenses in one month (appearing to indicate a serious problem), followed by euphoria a few months later when a major credit would come through.

The solution to this issue was to accrue the credit in the same month as the expense, based on the knowledge that we would receive reimbursement from the vendors. The figures then offset themselves *in the same month*. Suddenly, instead of having huge variances appear simply because of promotional expenses and reimbursements, any variance that appeared became something worth reacting to.

A few years ago I had an article published in *Inc.* magazine on this subject of making operating statements more informative. One of the delights of having articles published in a national magazine is that calls come in from around the country from people who find your insights particularly helpful and enlightening. One of these calls was from a man who was just exploding with excitement. After reading the article, he said he now felt empowered to solve a problem that had been plaguing him since the start of his business.

His business was renting plants to organizations for decorative purposes. The problem was if he had a great sales month and signed up a number of new accounts, his operating statement for the month showed the exact opposite story and said he had a financial disaster. This contradiction came about because his accountant said he had to immediately expense the newly purchased plants to support the new business, since the plants had only a ten month life span and couldn't be depreciated. The further irony was when he had a terrible month with very low sales, his operating statement perversely indicated that he had a terrific month. Why? Strong income from his established customer base with little or no offsetting expenses for new plants.

The solution was to simply amortize the cost of the plants over the 10 months in the operating statements, *regardless of what the accounting rule called for*. He now saw there was no reason to adhere to some accounting convention that simple common sense said was giving him patently bad information.

All off this may not seem very profound, but the failure to employ elementary accruals in such a manner can make operating statements useless.

Again, you need to take charge. If you are reacting to movements in expenses or receipts that you realize after analysis are the result of aberrations, ask if the intelligent use of accruals (that *you*—not the accountants—dictate) would clean up the report.

Summary

> ➤ Insist that your operating statements reflect what really happens in the business as you know it to be. It should not reflect someone else's view, regardless of their credentials or demands.

> ➤ Make sure the information is organized and displayed so trends, variances, and patterns jump off the page and alert you to the problem areas.

> ➤ If necessary, keep two sets of accounts—one for you, and one for the IRS that meets its requirements.

> ➤ When you spot an item that at first appears to require action, but in reality is an outgrowth of some aberration or accounting convention, explore whether the intelligent use of accruals can solve the problem.

The People Implications

The techniques and concepts at the heart of this book have far-ranging implications for both employees and management in virtually every organization.

Resistance to Change

The first implication has to do with the age-old problem of simply getting people to change. There is a normal tendency to resist change in any form. That resistance is even more pronounced when the change impacts behavior patterns. How employees and managers relate to data and information is definitely a behavior issue.

An article in the *Harvard Business Review* back in the 1960s discussed the problems of effecting change. The essence of the article was what we want to change can range from the trivial (a slight change in a printed form) to the profound (fundamental behavior changes). In fact, the author classified five levels of change across this spectrum.

The next point was that each level of change require a more comprehensive program to condition the organization for change at that level. Whereas the lowest level of change might require nothing more than a simple memo of instruction, each level beyond that demands a more comprehensive approach. Behavioral change is at the highest level of change and is analogous to a psychiatrist meeting with a patient. Typically, the psychiatrist and the patient need to meet twice a week for two years *at a minimum* in order to create significant behavior changes.

The problem in the business world is the tendency to attack all levels of change with a program valid only for the simplest type of change. Using a simple memo to attempt to institute far-reaching changes that will impact employees in the most profound sense isn't enough. The natural result is massive resistance. Yet management is bewildered. "These people sure are resistant to change. Why can't they see how good this new program is going to be?"

Throughout this book ways have been suggested in which you can fundamentally change your company's data and information environment. So far these changes have been technical and conceptional in nature. The fact is, though, that changes in the attitudes of people within your organization are just as important. For the technical and conceptional changes to stick, you must also provide your people with a program of training and familiarization that deals with the ideas described in this book.

Such training does not have to be lengthy, time-consuming, or highly technical. For example, people don't have to understand the inner workings of the system that triggers various exception reports—but they do have to understand the concept of looking only at the items that are behaving outside the normal range of variation. People are actually very good at grasping a concept without knowing all about the theory or mathematics behind it.

Such training could very easily use selected sections of this book as a text. If this training is augmented with actual examples from your own organization, the results could be extremely positive.

The key point is people must be introduced to these new concepts and approaches in a training environment before they begin using them. If they encounter them first as a sudden and dramatic change in their duties or responsibilities, they will naturally feel threatened—and will naturally resist.

How much training will your people need? That depends, of course, on how sweeping the changes are, how sharp your people are, and how clearly you can demonstrate that those changes will ultimately benefit both your organization and employees themselves. Typically, though, two to four two-hour sessions should be sufficient.

Management's Obligations

The new solutions, approaches, and concepts in this book ultimately strip away the "information fog" that envelops many organizations and allow management to focus attention on specific actionable events. For all its benefits, however, this new information environment can be abused by thoughtless or unscrupulous managers. Management has an obligation to ensure that the tools described in this book—particularly exception reports—are not used in a tyrannical way.

"Tyrannical?" you might ask. "Isn't that a bit extreme? How can a printed report become a tyrannical tool?"

As discussed earlier, for some time middle management has been partially shielded from upper management's scrutiny due to the inadequacies of the traditional information environment. Traditionally, middle managers have been asked highly general questions based on aggregated data, and they have been able to respond with equally general answers that may or may not have dealt with the problem.

Once new concepts and systems are put into place and you begin turning data into information, managers will be asked very specific questions about specific events. These are questions that have never been asked before— and they demand much clearer, more specific, and more rational responses. Furthermore, the inquiry they hear beneath each question could be, "How and why did you let this happen?" Or, to put it more bluntly, "Why did you screw up here?" Obviously this can create a potentially tense situation, but where does the tyranny come in?

It would be very easy for an executive, armed with a report that focused on very specific eye-opening events, to use it as a club on certain employees. This would be particularly true if the employee's initial responses to the executive's inquiries were vague and highly general—yet exactly the same answers that had previously been considered adequate.

The point is people not only need training to understand what they are dealing with, but also need some time to make the transition. *Management must resist any tendency to use this powerful system in a punitive or destructive way.*

Finally, middle managers have to be given tools that allow them to respond to the questions that arise. At a minimum, middle managers should be given the same information their superiors receive. This minimizes the opportunities for them to be blind-sided.

I have actually been in situations where upper management received some revealing information prior to anyone else in the organization. The executives quietly kept the information to themselves—then, in a staff meeting, started to ask pointed questions based on that information. Then they reveled in the confusion and embarrassment of their subordinates. Such an approach may do wonders for the egos of a few individuals, but it is catastrophic for both morale and the total organization.

A far better approach would be to outfit middle and lower management with comparable tools, but at even finer levels of detail. The sales tracking exception report is a good example. Executive management might receive a report that tracks the total sales level for each customer. Middle and lower management, however, might receive an exception report that tracks the same information but with the added level of detail *by product category*.

In this situation, executive management might ask the national sales manager, "What is going on with the Bonhoff Corporation? Their purchases last month took a terrific dip, well below any movement in the recent past." The sales manager would then be able to respond, "I noted that also, and it turns out that the drop was totally in the copper pipe product line. The other lines are holding up OK. When I asked Louise Compton, who handles the account, what was going on, she said we were blind-sided by Consolidated Reclaiming with some really low-ball prices. I have our product manager going out with Louise to the account to see if we can't convince them that in the longer run we are still their best bet."

Doesn't this sound far more constructive, and far more efficient, than a dumb look from the national sales manager, and the executive scoring a "gotcha"?

Summary

> The introduction of exception reports and other techniques is sufficiently revolutionary in its impact on employee behavior that it warrants a comprehensive, formal training program. This training program should include:

- Formal classroom-style sessions using this book as a text.

- Liberal use of examples from your own organization to make the concepts familiar and understandable.

➤ Resist any temptation to abuse lower management with information that represents a new level of insight before they have had a chance to adjust.

➤ Provide lower management with comparable tools that extract information at a level of detail equal to or greater than that provided to executive management.

The Role of Data and Information in Corporate Restructuring

For the past few years there has been a constant, and often strident, public discussion about the underlying causes of the downsizing and restructuring of corporate America. Foreign competition, worker displacement due to technology, corporate greed, new management concepts, and a variety of other explanations have been offered for this phenomenon. While there is no doubt that each of these forces has had some impact on the situation, there is something missing in all the standard explanations. Furthermore, none of the cited forces or trends explains the magnitude of the downsizing that occurs at many businesses. Why is it that, all of a sudden, a company can do very nicely without 20 percent of its middle management? That's one out of every five middle managers! This is analogous to suddenly being able to get by perfectly well on 20 percent less sleep—or 20 percent less income. Something must have been radically out of line for these major cutbacks to have few or no ill effects on organizations.

The missing element may have to do with a major revolution that has taken place in data and information handling.

Historically, a primary role of middle management has been as the processors and movers of data. Middle managers gathered data, organized and structured data, transmitted data, analyzed data, and on rare occasions turned some of it into information.

Starting in the late '50s, however, computers started to perform many of these same functions. This was gradual at first, but it grew at an ever-increasing rate, until by the '70s the process was in full swing. In the '80s the process had turned into an explosion of activity.

Throughout this period of change, however, companies really didn't change the way they were structured, or the way they dealt with these new processes and realities. Accordingly, many of the functions that middle management performed became redundant or superfluous. This was particularly true because middle management wasn't doing much to differentiate what they did from what computers were doing. Furthermore, they were not turning data into information.

An example that is relevant happened when I worked at the headquarters of U.S. Steel in the late '50s and early '60s. The company was then in its heyday, and it was highly regarded in the industry. Still, even as a young pup, the poverty of the process the company was calling analysis was clear to me. The various analysis groups, of which there were many, continually gathered, organized, and presented data. However, these groups had no real idea how to turn it into information. This failure to add value made them extremely vulnerable to the revolution that was brewing. If they *had* been turning the data into information the computers would have leveraged their efforts and made them more valuable than ever.

This same pattern that existed at U.S. Steel was being repeated over and over during the same period of time by many thousands of other companies—with more or less the same results.

Interestingly, as computers started to perform the functions of middle managers, there was no immediate reduction in headcount. In fact, as people become redundant in these functions, a certain self-perpetuation took place where one group made work for the other, and vice versa.

Then, in the late '80s, the mass lay offs started—and they became more pronounced in the '90s. These mass lay offs were analogous to what in physics is called a super-saturated solution. This is a phenomenon whereby a solution (a liquid containing some solids) is made to hold more of a particular solid than is normally possible at the existing temperature. If you were to drop even a tiny additional quantity of that solid material into the solution, a large quantity of that material would instantly, and very dramatically, solidify out of the solution.

This was the case with our corporate structures. Middle management was in a super-saturated state. Companies accepted the layers of management that no longer performed a meaningful function (and, in fact, were often in the way), simply because they *had always been there*. When the realization suddenly hit that these layers had to go, that key insight, and the lay offs that followed, took on many names—re-engineering, restructuring, downsizing, and so on. While some of the lay offs were excessive, by and large companies handled the new situation with little or no adverse effects. In fact, in many cases the elimination of management layers vastly improved their overall efficiency, and of course greatly lowered their cost of operations.

With this in mind, consider what will occur in the future when companies use the computer to create a true information environment. When businesses implement the techniques and approaches described in this book, there will likely be further major dismantling of much of what is left of middle management. The existing split that is already occurring in our labor force, between the technologically strong and the technologically weak, will accelerate, with all the unfortunate consequences. A large segment that has made it through the first wave of restructuring is still very vulnerable.

This vulnerability exists because managers are still not acting as converters of data into information. Their current functions are going to be completely usurped unless they are intellectually able to grasp the new concepts discussed in this book and turn them to their own use.

Who knows in which direction middle management will move? There is a strong chance that another wave of change is about to sweep over us, bringing with it tremendous upheaval for many people. Some specific individuals will benefit; many others will be harmed, at least in the short run. Society in general will benefit greatly in the long run, as it does any time we have a major breakthrough in efficiency.

Let this discussion be a clarion call, since people have choices in how they prepare themselves, how they respond to the challenge, and how they deal with change.

Summary

➤ Something has been overlooked behind the scenes regarding the recent trends of restructuring, re-engineering, and downsizing.

➤ For many years middle managers gathered data, organized and structured data, transmitted data, and analyzed data, but did not do a very good job of turning it into information. Thus they became vulnerable to the computer, and were ultimately displaced by it in large numbers.

➤ The downsizing process is going to be extended as we utilize concepts from this book and computers start to convert data into information.

➤ The managers who will prosper and survive in this new environment are those who embrace these new concepts and learn how to become a contributing part of the process.

Exception Reports for Accounts Receivables

Now it's time to return to the actual process of creating exception reports, and cover some specific areas beyond the earlier example of sales tracking.

This chapter, and the two that immediately follow, will show you how exception reports can be created for a variety of business concerns. These chapters will illustrate that, although the basic concepts are the same from application to application, certain modifications are required for each different area being tracked. While these chapters provide further insight into exception reporting concepts, feel free to skip any areas not applicable to your business, or that get into more detail than you need.

One of the articles I wrote some years ago for *Inc.* magazine focused on the subject of controlling accounts receivables. I started out somewhat whimsically by stating that "When I acquired Battery and Tire Warehouse our receivables were running about 52 days. Within a year under my brilliant management, that number was up to 60 days." To this day I cringe when I think about this early fiasco.

Our receivables situation worsened because of my failure to give the function my earnest attention and the management focus it deserved. Once I woke up to the situation, however, significant progress was made. Within another year the receivables were running just above the 30-day level, about as low as they could get in that industry.

It took a number of corrective actions to get this area under control, from replacing the credit manager through making changes in policies and procedures. A key area was making some sense out of the information and reporting process. With receivables, the old problem of data glut and information starvation was rampant.

Begin by reflecting on the reports that are traditionally available in the accounts receivable area.

First, there is the classic past due report, which can be from one to three inches thick, depending on the size of the company. In its traditional form, it is not organized to direct management attention to emerging problems. All the accounts are listed, whether there is something of significance for an account or not. Even more serious is the fact that only the most current status of each account is presented. Consequently, there is no perspective to the data, and there is no trend data from which to draw any conclusions. It's really just a snapshot of the current condition of each account.

The usual alternatives to the past due report are aggregate measurements of days of receivables, or the percent of the total accounts that are past due—both of which are fine for an overall indication of progress, but utterly useless for focusing attention on specific accounts.

In this chapter we will explore two innovative types of exception reports to help you convert the mass of data that typically exists in past due reports into highly structured information that will direct your attention to emerging and existing problem areas. These reports are not going to look exactly like the tools developed in earlier chapters. In fact, one purpose of this chapter is to illustrate the need to customize exception reports to the particular task at hand (though within a set of general principles).

You need to have two distinct mind-sets when managing accounts receivables, and you will generate a different type of exception report to address each set of concerns.

First, you should be concerned about the accounts where there has been a significant adverse change in the prior month—a change that is due to some negative event or condition, not normal random movement. You therefore want a report that will isolate these accounts as soon as this change occurs so that you can initiate action to minimize the potential of even greater problems in the future.

Secondly, and quite separately, you want to be alerted to the chronic problems—those accounts where there is a consistent and significant lack of payment, spanning a given time period. (But I am sure that you don't have any of these accounts, because I had them all!) These accounts require constant methodical action to force customers to address their chronic past due situations. You therefore want a report that will, first, prioritize these accounts so you can initially focus on the largest accounts with the highest cash exposure first, and then, second, constantly remind you of the state of your problem receivables so you do not tune out these messy problem areas.

Each type of report should isolate only the appropriate area of concern, and not commingle the two different classes of accounts, since each group needs to be approached with a different mind-set.

Significant Change Reports

The first challenge is to determine what to measure to determine if a significant change has occurred in any individual account. Since you are concerned with the past due status of the account, one approach could be to track the total dollars that are past due for the account, and have your computer trigger an exception when that amount goes outside the normal band of variation. The problem with using absolute sales dollars, however, is that the amount past due could vary greatly due to the sales activity in that particular account, rather than because of its payment activity. Consequently, you could get a false reading by tracking the absolute dollars only.

Instead track the past due dollars as a percent of each account's total receivables. Through experimentation this approach has proved to be more reliable than tracking the past due dollars alone.

Figure 11.1 on p. 88 illustrates one sample page from such a report. This is from an actual Battery and Tire Warehouse report (customer names have been changed).

The format here is similar to the conventional past due report, with "current balance" followed by "1 to 30 days past due," etc. Note that since we are generating an exception report, we are going to display only a small fraction of the accounts. We can now afford to display the trend of events by stacking the past five months of history under the current month. Immediately this enhances the value of the report. (One thing that drove me to distraction with conventional reports was that even when there was

Figure 11.1: A/R Significant Change Report

DSM Demo Company
April 1997

	Account Balance	Current	1 to 30 Days	31 to 60 Days	61 to 90 Days	91 Days & Over	Total $ Past Due	Percent Past Due
0025472 Anderson Inc. 321-2450 Our Rep #5								
Curr Mo	$4,281	$628	$3,653	$0	$0	$0	$3,653	85%
1st Prev.	$3,653	$3,653	$0	$0	$0	$0	$0	0%
2nd Prev.	$0	$0	$0	$0	$0	$0	$0	0%
3rd Prev.	$0	$0	$0	$0	$0	$0	$0	0%
4th Prev.	$1,229	$955	$274	$0	$0	$0	$274	22%
5th Prev.	$1,728	$1,229	$499	$0	$0	$0	$499	29%
0026385 Adrian Inc. 453-9867 Our Rep #9								
Curr Mo	$7,333	$4,498	$2,835	$0	$0	$0	$2,835	39%
1st Prev.	$5,569	$5,569	$0	$0	$0	$0	$0	0%
2nd Prev.	$3,139	$3,139	$0	$0	$0	$0	$0	0%
3rd Prev.	$4,152	$4,152	$0	$0	$0	$0	$0	0%
4th Prev.	$1,229	$338	$0	$0	$0	$0	$0	0%
5th Prev.	$3,531	$2,531	$0	$0	$0	$0	$0	0%
0026385 Akkers Hauling Inc 453-9856 Our Rep #5								
Curr Mo	$4,595	$1,900	$1,520	$1,157	$16	$0	$2,693	59%
1st Prev.	$2,694	$2,039	$157	$333	$163	$0	$653	24%
2nd Prev.	$2,654	$2,194	$333	$553	$173	$0	$1,059	40%
3rd Prev.	$3,460	$2,379	$953	$127	$0	$0	$1,080	31%
4th Prev.	$4,080	$3,929	$635	$515	$0	$0	$1,150	28%
5th Prev.	$4,150	$2,672	$937	$539	$0	$0	$1,476	36%

an account of interest, only a snapshot of the most recent month was displayed, and there was no way to track the pattern of events that preceded the current situation.)

On the far right of the significant change report is the percent of the total receivables that is past due. This is the criterion the system will monitor and use as the basis to trigger the exception. When the current figure is outside the normal band of variation, the account will be selected for display.

Note the second account, Adrian Inc. You might well exclaim, "What is the mystery here? The company has been current all along and then went past due. I don't need fancy statistics to isolate this account." True—but now look at the third account, Akkers Hauling. This customer has been consistently past due—but in the current month its past due situation went outside its prior band of experience. Clearly, even though Akkers Hauling has been a consistent problem, its payment situation has deteriorated significantly in the current month and warrants prompt management attention.

As part of the design of this report, you should create a summary page that totals the figures in two ways. Figure 11.2 on p. 90 displays an example of such a summary. Note that the first block of figures represents the totals for only the 37 accounts selected as exceptions. The format across the page is the same as the detail report. The bottom block of figures simply presents totals for all accounts. Note there are 3,791 accounts on file, with a past due distribution as shown across the page. (This example also comes from real data and a real business situation, not theory. Company names have been changed.)

This summary report highlights the power of the exception system that has been created. There are two key observations to bring to your attention.

First, note only 37 accounts were triggered out of a total of 3,791, or less than 1 percent. (Not all companies will have this dramatic a ratio, but the percent of accounts displayed will still be very low—usually well under 5 percent.) This represents a tremendous compression of data down to vital information.

This compression would be of little value if the items highlighted by the exception report did not account for virtually all of the problem areas. Test that concern with our second observation.

Note that in the 1-to-30 Days past due column, the total accounts improved over the previous month by $29,043 ($133,113 − $104,070). This is certainly a desirable trend, and indicates a bona fide reduction in money owed. On the surface we could conclude that all is well and pur-

FIGURE 11.2: A/R Significant Change Summary Report

DSM Demo Company
April 1997

	Account Balance	Current	1 to 30 Days	31 to 60 Days	61 to 90 Days	91 Days & Over	Total $ Past Due	Percent Past Due
37 Problem Accounts Selected								
Curr Mo	$164,385	$79,211	$47,306	$21,736	$7,854	$8,542	$85,438	52%
1st Prev.	$133,137	$74,311	$34,635	$13,584	$3,254	$7,514	$58,987	44%
2nd Prev.	$104,596	$64,149	$24,928	$6,744	$4,698	$5,544	$41,914	40%
3rd Prev.	$90,763	$58,767	$17,720	$9,266	$2,541	$1,745	$31,272	34%
4th Prev.	$80,125	$39,736	$27,571	$11,476	$608	$1,085	$40,740	51%
5th Prev.	$112,584	$65,274	$27,858	$15,666	$4,458	$1,454	$49,436	44%
3791 Accounts (All Accounts)								
Curr Mo	$1,264,871	$1,025,321	$104,070	$25,869	$13,698	$109,456	$253,093	20%
1st Prev.	$1,192,689	$902,546	$133,113	$39,568	$16,548	$111,458	$300,687	25%
2nd Prev.	$985,288	$644,586	$187,542	$33,444	$25,465	$99,456	$345,907	35%
3rd Prev.	$1,082,142	$822,787	$117,856	$44,569	$38,569	$68,789	$269,783	25%
4th Prev.	$1,096,525	$785,421	$188,548	$58,478	$26,548	$70,125	$343,699	31%
5th Prev.	$1,278,452	$941,586	$213,569	$50,125	$23,564	$68,987	$356,245	28%

sue the issue no further. Note, however, that for the 37 exception accounts there was a $12,671 *increase* in dollars 1-to-30 days past due, from $34,635 to $47,306.

Think of the implications of this! While the overall situation has been improving, there are nevertheless 37 specific accounts that are notably deteriorating. The system, however, managed to reach into the mass of data and extract these specific accounts for observation and corrective action.

This is the classic situation that occurs with business data all the time: the aggregates look fine, but buried in the detail are problem situations that we could—and should—act upon at an early stage, if only we could detect those problems.

Chronic Problem Reports

The next area of concern is the chronic problem accounts. These are the accounts that, despite your best efforts, have deteriorated into a situation of chronic non-payment. You may wish to still work with some of the accounts, or even sell to them on a C.O.D. basis, but you will nevertheless need to keep the pressure on—and, more important, make sure that the accounts don't deteriorate further.

Figure 11.3 on p. 92 is an example of a chronic problem report on the same customers shown earlier. In this case the system has isolated only those accounts where there has been chronic non-payment or under-payment. The format of the report is similar to Figure 11.1, except that we have added two columns to the far right.

The first such column, "% 30+ Days Past Due," indicates the percentage of total receivables for an account that is past due 30 days or more. This figure will be used, as well as the total amount past due, to isolate the most troublesome accounts. (The column at the very far right will be discussed shortly.)

You can use the two percentages at the far right to begin to identify which of your accounts qualify for the chronic problem exception report. In Figure 11.3, an account is identified as a possible candidate for the report when at least 70 percent of the account balance is past due (column eight) and at least 20 percent of the balance is 30 or more days past due.

Another device has been added to our example for an account to appear on the exception report, it must meet the two criteria above for two consecutive months. Conversely, if the account manages to stay under one or both criteria for a month, it comes off the report—and only goes back on if it meets both criteria for two consecutive months again.

These numbers are of course not absolutes. You should experiment with any or all of them—both the percentage cutoffs and the number of consecutive months—to design your own chronic problem report for your particular business.

Chronic problem reports need one additional criterion to be most useful: a minimum dollar figure for receivables. This screens out the trivial

FIGURE 11.3: A/R Chronic Problem Report

DSM Demo Company
April 1997

	Account Balance	Current	1 to 30 Days	31 to 60 Days	61 to 90 Days	91 Days & Over	Total $ Past Due	Total % Past Due	% 30+Days Past Due	# Months On Rpt.
004442 Franklin Motors 433-2501 Our Rep #5										
Curr Mo	$2,657	$36	$36	$80	$2,505	$0	$2,621	99%	97%	1
1st Prev.	$2,621	$36	$80	$2,505	$0	$0	$2,585	99%	96%	
2nd Prev.	$2,585	$80	$2,505	$0	$0	$0	$2,505	97%	0%	
3rd Prev.	$2,505	$2,505	$0	$0	$0	$0	$0	0%	0%	
4th Prev.	$567	$567	$0	$0	$0	$0	$0	0%	0%	
5th Prev.	$140	$140	$0	$0	$0	$0	$0	0%	0%	
0045879 M & T Tire Service 456-4567 Our Rep #4										
Curr Mo	$2,173	$1,045	$0	$0	$0	$1,128	$1,128	52%	52%	9+
1st Prev.	$1,128	$0	$0	$0	$89	$1,039	$1,128	100%	100%	
2nd Prev.	$1,228	$18	$0	$89	$0	$1,121	$1,210	99%	99%	
3rd Prev.	$1,410	$20	$108	$0	$0	$1,282	$1,390	99%	91%	
4th Prev.	$1,390	$108	$0	$0	$0	$1,282	$1,282	92%	92%	
5th Prev.	$1,351	$20	$0	$0	$0	$1,331	$1,331	99%	99%	
0024785 Sandler Transportation Inc. 453-9456 Our Rep #5										
Curr Mo	$9,850	$978	$133	$139	$144	$8,456	$8,872	90%	89%	14
1st Prev.	$10,269	$1,103	$139	$144	$8	$8,875	$9,166	89%	88%	
2nd Prev.	$10,544	$1,845	$144	$8	$0	$8,547	$8,699	83%	81%	
3rd Prev.	$10,985	$1,540	$139	$0	$678	$8,628	$9,445	86%	85%	
4th Prev.	$10,674	$1,368	$0	$678	$2,236	$6,392	$9,306	87%	87%	
5th Prev.	$11,360	$1,204	$744	$2,207	$4,168	$3,037	$10,156	89%	83%	

accounts. (In Figure 11.3 an account balance of $500 was used as a minimum. It's not that anything under that figure is meaningless, but the report didn't need to be cluttered up with trivia that obscured where the big bucks, and big problems, were.) You will of course need to set a minimum balance due that's most appropriate for your own business and accounts.

To the far right of Figure 11.3 you will note the column "Number Months On Rpt." This is a simple count of the number of consecutive months that each problem account has appeared on the exception report. Note that the last account, Sandler Transportation, has been on the report for 14 months. (You may wonder why was the company putting up with an account that was this chronically delinquent. Actually, Sandler was on C.O.D. plus 10 percent, meaning that shipments would only be made if they paid for product at the time of receipt, plus an additional 10 percent to be applied against their old balance. Knowing that the two exception reports would immediately trigger attention should the account regress, I felt free to pursue this policy.)

This consecutive months figure gives additional perspective to the account—and demonstrates immediately and graphically just how chronic a problem it is. Its a brutal reminder and attention-getter in an area that has significant financial implications.

One additional piece of information can be added to the figures in this column. Adding a plus sign after the number of months, as with M & T Tire Service, can indicate that the total balance in the account (aside from past due charges) has risen since the last report—in other words, further orders have been accepted without immediate payment. This means that somehow a salesperson caused us to increase our exposure with an account that was already defined as a chronic problem—a major violation of policy on the salesperson's part.

If I had only five minutes at the end of the month to worry about accounts receivables, at minimum I would look for the plus signs in the chronic problem report and ask some pertinent questions.

Figure 11.4 on p. 94 is a summary report, similar in concept to what you looked at earlier for the significant change area.

The lower block of figures contains the same information that appeared as part of Figure 11.2, the significant change summary report—with the

FIGURE 11.4: A/R Chronic Problem Summary Report

DSM Demo Company
April 1997

42 Chronic Problem Accounts Selected

	Account Balance	Current	1 to 30 Days	31 to 60 Days	61 to 90 Days	91 Days & Over	Total $ Past Due	Total % Past Due	% 30+ Days Past Due
Curr Mo	$175,221	$27,728	$6,969	$19,387	$12,160	$108,977	$147,493	84%	80%
1st Prev.	$165,956	$5,175	$26,402	$19,509	$13,926	$100,944	$160,781	97%	81%
2nd Prev.	$176,228	$12,989	$21,944	$20,720	$21,565	$99,010	$163,239	93%	80%
3rd Prev.	$177,616	$20,041	$26,404	$27,835	$35,337	$67,999	$157,575	89%	74%
4th Prev.	$206,876	$38,216	$35,200	$42,772	$24,470	$66,218	$168,660	82%	65%
5th Prev.	$212,691	$40,578	$49,806	$40,121	$18,198	$63,988	$172,113	81%	58%

3791 Accounts (All Accounts)

	Account Balance	Current	1 to 30 Days	31 to 60 Days	61 to 90 Days	91 Days & Over	Total $ Past Due	Total % Past Due	% 30+ Days Past Due
Curr Mo	$1,264,871	$1,025,321	$104,070	$25,869	$13,698	$109,456	$253,093	20%	12%
1st Prev.	$1,192,689	$902,546	$133,113	$39,568	$16,548	$111,458	$300,687	25%	14%
2nd Prev.	$985,288	$644,586	$187,542	$33,444	$25,465	$99,456	$345,907	35%	16%
3rd Prev.	$1,082,142	$822,787	$117,856	$44,569	$38,569	$68,789	$269,783	25%	14%
4th Prev.	$1,096,525	$785,421	$188,548	$58,478	$26,548	$70,125	$343,699	31%	14%
5th Prev.	$1,278,452	$941,586	$213,569	$50,125	$23,564	$68,987	$356,245	28%	11%

addition of an extra column to the far right showing the percent of the total account balance that is more than 30 days past due.

The top block represents the totals for the 42 accounts that were extracted as chronic problems. Note again the very small percentage of the accounts that were extracted (just over 1 percent)—but also note how they constitute virtually all of the dollars owed that are 60 or more days past due.

Management Action and Focus

These reports changed the entire method of managing the accounts receivables function at Battery and Tire Warehouse. Rather than poring over an 80-page past due report into a state of numbness, the focus was instantly on the key problem areas as they emerged.

In addition, these reports changed the entire tone of the dialog with others in the organization. Rather than asking aggregated questions and getting back aggregated answers that said nothing, I was asking pointed, specific questions on how a specific situation came about. "How come our exposure went up at M&T when they have been a chronic problem?"

The specific problem was not as interesting to me as what flaw in the system or violation of policy caused it to happen. Being able to identify these situations as they occurred and move in quickly, the entire organization tightened up and operated more efficiently.

In fact, employees quickly started to realize that every time a policy was violated, somehow shortly thereafter the people involved were asked specific questions and being held accountable. Eventually, it became easier for everyone to follow company policies and stop the inefficient short-cuts.

Summary

- ➤ The accounts receivables function lends itself well to monitoring via exception reports, with major positive results.

- ➤ Accounts receivables illustrate the need to innovate so the correct criteria are used to extract the exception items.

- ➤ Two types of exception reports work well in this function:

- Significant change reports, which isolate accounts whose past due positions have noticeably deteriorated.
- Chronic problem reports, which isolate the relatively few accounts where there is chronic non-payment or underpayment.

➤ At the end of each report, a summary page can illustrate the relatively few exceptions account for virtually all of the collection problems.

➤ Availability of these reports radically changes the way you communicate with your subordinates and allows you to focus on specific problem events rather than vague generalities.

Exception Reports in Inventory Management

This chapter deals with the specific area of managing inventories. It is of interest for two reasons. First, it will provide how-to ideas for applying exception reports in this area. Second, it will introduce a new set of selection criteria that will further stimulate your thoughts on how this concept of exception reporting can work in a variety of settings.

By now you should see a pattern of how to devise a set of exception reports for a given area. The first step is *always* to stand back and ask what the really critical issues are that you want to track—and what specific problems or situations you want to be alerted to. In sales you will be most concerned with accounts that are exhibiting a significant deterioration in sales levels. In accounts receivables, you will want to identify accounts that exhibit a significant adverse change in the current month's past due status, as well as any chronically past due accounts. For the inventory management area, you are interested in the stock status of the stock keeping units (SKUs) in your inventory. But you are not really interested in the stock status of *every* item or SKU, just the ones that are calling out for action—in other words, the exceptions.

In managing inventories, there are two basic situations that require management action. The first relates to items that are in excess supply—you have too much inventory for the expected sales level of the item. These items will appear on a **slow moving report**. Excess inventory is an actionable condition; you should be taking positive steps to move this inventory, rather than waiting for normal expected demand to reduce it over time.

The second actionable situation is the exact opposite. You need to be made aware of items that are in danger of going out of stock before the replenishment order is due to arrive. These items will appear on your **hot report**. Unless you take expediting action, you will be out of stock of these items and will damage your customer satisfaction performance.

Note that you are ignoring *all* the items in the middle – every item where there is sufficient stock to meet anticipated demand, yet not so much stock that idle capital is tied up uselessly. It is hoped that these items you are ignoring constitute the vast preponderance of your SKUs. You should be hopeful because many inventories are so out of balance that the exceptions come close to outnumbering the non-exceptions.

You must of course come up with a criterion you can use to isolate your exceptions. What is going to identify something that is slow moving or, conversely, something that is moving so fast it is dangerously close to being out of stock? The answer will be the number of months' supply on hand for each individual item or SKU.

Months' supply is easily calculated by taking the quantity on hand and dividing it by the forecast of future monthly demand. For example, if you have 67 items in stock and a monthly forecast for the item of 39, then you have 1.7 months' supply (67 divided by 39). While a little high, 1.7 months of stock is a reasonable quantity to have on hand and most likely would not be considered an exception requiring special action.

Accurately forecasting future demand is critical. Unless your forecast is reasonably accurate, the resulting number of months' supply will not mean much. Suffice it to say that the forecasting technique you use must have some statistical reliability.

Slow Moving Report

Once your software has calculated the months' supply on hand for each SKU, the process of creating a slow moving report becomes very simple.

Here's how a software system could create a customized slow moving report. You click on the icon requesting this report. The system prompts you to declare which group of SKUs you wish to examine for the report. You may wish to see a report for the entire inventory, for products from only one vendor, or for items from only one warehouse location.

Then the system asks you for the number of months' supply you want to use as a cut-off. For example, you may wish to see only the items where you have 10 months' supply or greater. (This flexibility allows you to look initially at only the worst situations for action. Then, as you get these situations under control, you can start to tighten down on the criterion.)

The final report looks similar to Figure 12.1, which provides the number of items on hand, the monthly forecast, and the number of months' supply in inventory. Here the cut-off has been set at seven months' supply.

FIGURE 12.1: **Example of a Slow Moving Report**

Slow Moving Report
All Vendors—Atlanta Warehouse Only
2/12/1997

Item Number	Item Description	On-Hand	Per Month Forecast	Months' Supply
AX00543	Holder – ¾"	45	2	12.0+
BRX456	Elbow – Cu-½"	243	23	10
BX-3492	Coupling – Cu-1"	8	0	12.0+
C345234	Hose-X Type – ½"	34	4	8.5

There is one additional criterion that you may want to add to the system: the number of months that you want to have pass after an item is initially stocked before it can be considered slow moving. The purpose behind this extra check is to eliminate items that were just recently introduced, and for which inventory was stocked in anticipation of sales. With this extra check, the item is given a chance to move (and therefore to start creating a valid forecast) before the computer can bring it to anyone's attention as slow moving. (Two months is a good default figure here.)

Note how much more effective this report is than a report based on the *age* of the product. (Many so-called exception reports isolate items that are over a given number of months in age.) Why wait until an item is 12 months old before triggering it for action? Our report triggers it for action even if it is new product that somehow ended up in stock despite insufficient demand.

Once again, this report enables you to ask pointed questions that relate to specific events. Rather than asking vague general questions based on highly aggregated data, you are pinpointing specific areas of interest and asking highly specific questions.

When I first starting using this type of exception report at Battery and Tire Warehouse, there was the same rapid transformation in our internal communication that we had in other areas. For example, I was now able to ask, "How come we are sitting on 21 of these truck tires? That's a 12-month supply."

A very credible answer might be: "Well, Cox Freight asked for 18 on a special order, and when they arrived they didn't like the tread design and turned them down. Considering what a big account they are, I went along with it and put them into inventory."

"What are we doing about those tires now, however?"

"I'm checking with Freizer Haulers to see if they'll take them at our inventory cost. They aren't too picky on tread designs and will be interested in a good deal."

This is a great dialog. The exception report highlighted the problem. The investigation indicated there was no violation of policy, and the follow-up action was quite sensible.

Compare this to the following conversation, also from actual experience:

"What are we doing with 38 of these tires? We've got a 14-month supply!"

"Oh, they're logger tires. I brought them in because Joe, our dealer up in Duluth, said they should be a great opportunity this fall."

"Wait a minute. Did we check with the sales guys up there? Besides, Joe is notorious for giving the kind of advice that never pans out. As long as he doesn't have to carry the inventory personally he'll suggest anything. Let's be clear that we don't operate this way, OK? Now let's start figuring out how to limit the damage by contacting the Duluth sales rep."

This is a great demonstration of another use of the report. The situation was highlighted almost immediately after the product arrived. A violation of policy was determined and acted upon. The problem was addressed—and a solution sought—while the product was still fresh and the situation new.

Hot Report

For your hot report you should normally deal in *days'* supply rather than months, since you are interested in a much shorter time period. (This can simply be the months' supply multiplied by 30.5.)

Again, you will go through the process of how a software system could generate this report. After clicking on the icon for a hot report, you are given the opportunity to select the group of SKUs in question. Then the system asks how many days' supply you want as a cut-off. (If you key in 10 days, for example, the system then looks for all the SKUs for which the on-hand balance is less than 10 days, and prints a report similar to Figure 12.2.)

Just prior to creating the report the system asks you one additional question: "Do you want the on-order amount to be added to the on-hand?" This extra step allows you to eliminate items where there may be, say, only six days' supply on hand, but where product is on order and will arrive prior to the total depletion of existing stock. (Once again, we are constantly attempting to make sure that every item on the exception report has a valid basis for action, and is not a "gee whiz" item.)

FIGURE 12.2: Example of a Hot Report

Hot Report
10 Days' Supply or Less
All Vendors – Atlanta Warehouse Only
2/12/1997

Item Number	Item Description	On-Hand	On-Order	Committed To Customers	Monthly Forecast	Days' Supply
AZ03543	Snap – 1¾"	3	5	0	29	8.4
DRX44556	Elbow – Cu-½"	0	15	6	19	4.7
GBX-93492	Pipe – Cu-1"	8	0	0	32	7.6
HQ395234	Hose – Neo-¼"	0	0	0	4	0.0

Note again how this report is so much more effective than the classic out of stock report, which passes for an exception report in many systems. Once you are out of stock the battle is already lost. At best you are being reactive to a bad situation. In a hot report, however, you are being alerted *prior* to the problem and given a chance to be proactive.

If you are interested in a more detailed and thorough discussion of inventory management, consult my first book, **A New Era In Inventory Management.** (See the reference at the end of this book for ordering information.)

Summary

➤ Inventory management is an area that is very conducive to exception reporting.

➤ Develop a criterion of months' supply, or days' supply, for selection of exceptions.

➤ Create a **slow moving report** that isolates the items that, regardless of age, are overstocked and require special action to move them out of inventory.

➤ Create a **hot report** that isolates the items that are in danger of being out of stock before replenishment stock is due to arrive.

The Role of the Computer

In today's business world, your computer will create all of the different exception reports that have been discussed. You may elect to have this function programmed into your existing software system, in which case you would have a new program that accesses the various data banks, such as sales history, accounts receivable, inventory status, etc.

The actual programming is relatively straightforward, and most of the effort qualifies as data processing. The algorithms that track the various items such as the exponential average and mean absolute deviation are a little more complex, but they are also straightforward calculations. Any competent, reasonably experienced programmer will be able to program these concepts into your computer.

Another approach is possible—and for some businesses preferable. This is to create a separate system on an independent personal computer that accesses the data via a download program and then processes the information off-line. This approach has two advantages. First, it takes the computation burden off your primary computer, thereby ensuring that its performance of other tasks is not affected. Second, by shifting the data and the processing to the PC, the entire function can be programmed to operate in a Windows environment, with all the excellent graphics that are available with little or no effort. Basically, this approach creates a quasi-client server operation.

While you can of course design and implement your own such system, by the time you read this book I may have developed a commercial product that offers these capabilities. It will be a stand-alone PC application and will be similar to one that I created, called MARS-95, to implement the concept and theories from my inventory management book, **A New Era in Inventory Management**. (See the reference at the end of the book for additional information.)

This new system will be designed to create action-oriented exception reports consistent with the theories discussed earlier. It will download data from all the areas that have a direct bearing on an organization's profits: sales, gross margins, receivables, inventory status, customer fill rates, return experience, vendor performance (covering both fill rates and lead time consistency), warehouse performance, etc. Then the PC will screen this data to determine what specific areas are exhibiting significant movement, and thus require management attention and action.

In the years to come, commercial systems will surely become available that offer similar functions for other areas of business. Imagine what these systems can do. You arrive in the morning and call up your Vital Signs Exception System. Instantly, your screen reveals *only the areas that deserve your attention.*

You can then call up a graphic display of any specific item to see more clearly why the system flagged it—and to add that special insight only the human mind can impart when looking at graphically displayed data. Then, if you like, you can drill down into backup data to see if any additional factors or patterns emerge. Armed with specific quantitative information, you are now in an ideal position to contact people closer to the situation and deal directly with the problem.

Is this starting to sound like some of the promises made early in this book?

Summary

- ➤ The programming required to generate exception reports is quite straightforward, and can be written by virtually any competent, experienced programmer.

- ➤ You may take one of two approaches:

  - Program the logic directly into your primary computer software, or

  - Create a separate Windows-oriented PC-based system that downloads the data and turns it into information off-line—thus freeing your main computer of the computational load.

From Information to Knowledge to Wisdom

Turning data into information is really just one step in the more expansive process of acquiring knowledge and wisdom. Each process can be defined as follows:

Data is made up of measurements and observations.

Information results when data is processed to extract particular items that focus our attention and trigger a specific reaction. This reaction may be active—changing a procedure or asking a particular employee about a certain account—or it may be more passive, in that we add it to our body of knowledge for future use.

Knowledge is a body of organized information that enables us to effectively generalize and predict. Knowledge exists when information starts to impart truths, or we begin to come to general conclusions as a result of our information gathering.

Wisdom is a state that transcends its roots of information and knowledge. With wisdom, the mind has correlated a body of knowledge and developed accurate mental models that are valid beyond the original information and knowledge sources. Wisdom is not merely knowing something, but understanding what it means, how it fits into the larger context, and how to act wisely on it.

Take the example of sales data and track it through these definitions.

The original measurements of sales dollars by customer for the last several months constitute **data.**

When you subject that data to the methods discussed throughout this book, isolating the areas that require action and showing why this action is necessary, you now have **information**.

When you know the events that are related to this information— you know *why* the sales of a certain account went down—you have **knowledge**.

When you have developed a body of knowledge and experience in the general area of sales and know how to reliably act on it to achieve an objective, you have attained **wisdom**.

No one can provide a rigorous system for making the move from information to knowledge to wisdom. In this chapter, however, there are some useful observations on the subject. In the following examples, anecdotes, and situations, I offer insights gleaned from over 40 years in the business world, in contexts ranging from a small entrepreneurial environment to Fortune 500 companies.

There is one consistent theme to the concepts presented in the following pages. All have the primary purpose of ensuring we take the information we have gathered and translate it into wise actions—*actions which are free of any destructive emotional content.*

All too often, people (myself included) will do a respectable job of gathering information and acquiring knowledge, only to let some unrelated or misplaced emotional reaction hinder the process of turning it into wisdom. The examples and case histories that follow will demonstrate ways in which management can respond as wisely, constructively, and appropriately as possible in a wide range of circumstances.

Turn off the Faucet

According to an old story, a small town in Vermont was faced with a dilemma concerning a resident who was acting oddly. The town leaders thought he might have some mental impairment, but they weren't sure. How should they decide whether or not he was mentally stable?

They finally came up with a simple screening test. They put him in a room where a sink was full and overflowing, and a faucet was running. They gave him a mop and told him to mop up the floor. The town leaders figured that if he turned off the faucet, he was probably pretty sane—but if he busily mopped the floor while leaving the faucet running, he had a problem.

This story may make you chuckle, particularly at the absurdity of mopping up while a sink is overflowing. But in business, unfortunately, there is a *consistent* tendency to mop the floor with the faucet running! Endless systems are in place that are specifically there to address the problems caused by flawed systems that are in place somewhere else.

Furthermore, managers often choose to keep solving recurring problems that emanate from the same source—while the obvious solution is to find out what is flawed in the first place and correct the problem at its source. (In other words, turn off the faucet!)

Generally the necessary information is in hand regarding an issue—and often the knowledge of the problem's roots—but the next step hasn't been taken of applying wisdom by taking broader corrective action.

This principle sounds obvious, but in real-life situations it isn't often used—in part because in the real world, problems tend to be complicated. The same problem may not always present itself in the same way each time, so it is not always apparent that it emanates from the same source. In addition, it often seems a lot easier to solve the immediate problem than to get at the source and correct it there. The fact that in the long run we would be *miles* ahead if we examined and corrected the source gets lost in the rush of current events.

A classic example occurred at Battery and Tire Warehouse. There was a chronic problem of "mis-pulls," where the warehouse workers would occasionally pick the wrong product from the bins and ship it to the customer. A mis-pull had horrible implications. Not only was the customer unhappy, but the product had to be brought back, a credit issued, the correct product pulled, and an invoice reissued. It was nothing but trouble and added expense. Yet somehow the periodic mis-pulls were accepted as just part of the business—a dripping faucet that couldn't be turned off.

Faced with the prospect of a never-ending sequence of mopping up after blunders, I initiated a program to locate the root causes of mis-pulls. The plan was to obtain data about the mis-pulls that I could transform first into information, then into knowledge.

Three causes were quickly identified: poor lighting, similar-looking items stored next to one another, and employee uncertainty about bin locations. Once the problems were precisely identified they weren't difficult to fix. The lighting in the warehouse was improved to enhance employees' ability to see pick tickets and product labels. (Obvious, you say. Don't bet on it! The lighting level had been universally accepted *for years* as perfectly adequate.) The bin locations were also printed on the pick tickets, and items that were easily confused were moved into bins were not adjacent. The net effect was that the faucet had been turned off. The incidence of mis-pulls dropped dramatically.

Incidentally, if I had kept the company longer, I would have eventually instituted a system of pulling product based on bar coding, which would have put the final lock on the faucet that still had an occasional drip.

The key to this entire process is to resist the temptation to make a quick fix. You have to have the discipline to step back and go after the root causes of the problem—i.e., to follow the process through the information stage to knowledge. Your information becomes knowledge when you realize that the problems have a pattern, and are the result of something that is flawed. While you do usually need to fix the immediate problem, you need to break the syndrome (both in yourself and in others) of saying, "This is simply the way it is." Moreover, you need the discipline to take the time to fix the problem for good— rather than let yourself deal with its symptoms over and over.

Popularize the metaphor of "turn off the faucet!" in your own organization. It's an easily-grasped idea that everyone can relate to. In fact, the analogy is so strong, and the implications of mopping the floor with the faucet running so insulting, that they tend to galvanize action. After all, how can you continue to mop after someone has pointed out that you have not checked the faucet?

There is an important variant of this concept called the **broken faucet syndrome**. In this case, everyone not only accepts that a faucet is running, but also buys into the belief that it's broken and can't be fixed. On top of all this, they add the following thought: "and there is nothing we can do about it except mop up afterward."

The classic example of this syndrome is a system that is put in place solely to compensate for someone in the company not doing the job the way it should be done.

Here is an example from my own experience. In the company I was running, somebody in management spent part of each day checking over purchase orders generated by the city desk. I asked why, and was told, "Oh, you have to because the guys at the city desk never bother to follow procedures, and besides, they are sloppy."

After scraping myself off the ceiling, I decided to find out why my city desk employees weren't following procedures.

Often, there is a good reason why people ignore procedures. For example, the procedures themselves may be badly flawed—but if that is the case, then management needs to develop new procedures (ideally in consultation with some of the people who will be following them). Once reasonable procedures are in place, then it becomes what I like to call "a condition of employment" that people follow the system. No company can tolerate what amounts to anarchy.

With my city desk situation, I first started to gather some data to isolate if we had a specific problem with one or two individuals, or if the sloppiness was across the board. The data illustrated the problem was fairly random, which then led to follow-up discussions with the city desk people themselves, using actual examples of bad paperwork that had caused specific problems later in the process. The discussions clearly indicated we did have some clumsy procedures—but the biggest issue was that the city desk employees simply were oblivious to the full implications of their sloppy work. The problem disappeared very quickly once we addressed the clumsy procedures. (This had the added benefit of letting the city desk employees know that more was being done than just leaning on them.) We also held a short training session on both the new procedures and the implications of bad paperwork in this particular area.

As I look back on my career as a manager, I can see that this constant drive to turn off the faucet resulted over and over in tremendous efficiencies. Once the faucets were turned off, I was spending less and less time on the actual day-to-day business operations. The proper systems and procedures were in place, and they were being followed.

What Are You Trying to Achieve?

Some time ago I had a very competent controller who was outstanding technically, and 100 percent conscientious in every sense. He had less than outstanding people skills, however. One day I overheard him raking our accounts payable clerk over the coals. Later on I asked him, "What were you trying to achieve with your conversation with Jane this morning? It sounded like you were going at it hot and heavy."

"Oh, I was trying get it through her head that she had to shape up and start doing her job more carefully."

I replied, "What you did would have made more sense to me if you were trying to humiliate her, or destroy her sense of self-worth, or create a tremendous sense of resentment, because that's what it sounded like to me."

This fellow was a sound person at heart, and he had to admit that if he really wanted to motivate the clerk, browbeating her was not only not appropriate, but tremendously counterproductive.

I suspect that my controller, at the moment of being abusive, actually wanted to unload his emotional frustration. In a sense he wanted to make himself feel better. Yet once he flushed up to the surface what he *should* be trying to achieve, his actions did not match up with reality.

This question "What are you trying to achieve?" is one of my most important sanity checks. Often there is no sync between what we are trying to achieve and what we are really doing. We have the necessary information and knowledge for the situation, but our emotions get in the way of doing what truly makes sense.

Colin Powell's outstanding autobiography, made it clear that throughout his life he operated by asking himself this question over and over again. This was particularly apparent in the way he handled the racial humiliations and insults that were an inevitable part of his life, especially when he was assigned to Army bases in the Deep South in the 1950s and 1960s Since his absolute single-minded commitment was to rise in the military hierarchy, he time and time again was careful not to throw himself away in a gesture of defiance that may have killed his long-run objectives. As a result of his attaining those objectives, Powell has had a more positive and profound long-term impact on the lives of African-Americans than any legitimate (but perhaps futile) protest would have.

This concept of asking yourself what you are trying to achieve sounds so simple you may tend to dismiss it. Test it out on yourself a few times, however. It is, at base, yet another way of turning data into information and then knowledge.

Having the information and even the knowledge doesn't do you much good if something intervenes and blocks it from becoming wisdom. You must align your actions with your goals, or the entire process will have been futile.

Apply the Principles of Triage

During World War II, the carnage on the battlefield totally overwhelmed field hospitals, resulting in a devastating loss of life. In response, a French surgeon came up with a brilliant suggestion that was dubbed **triage**. The theory was that, after a major battle, the mass of injured soldiers at a field hospital broke into three groups. The first group were likely going to die, regardless of what the doctors did. The second group were going to eventually get better, regardless of what wasn't done. The third was the group where medical intervention could make all the difference. This group, the surgeon said, was where the limited resources should be concentrated.

There is something brutally logical and efficient about this concept, and in many ways it offends our sensibilities. A soldier with both arms broken cries out for attention—but in reality, he will be virtually certain to live, and the arms can be set later, despite an interim cost in pain and suffering. Conversely, the soldier with massive internal bleeding who is in shock may have an outside chance of survival if given a tremendous amount of care, but that same care allocated to soldiers in the third group has a much higher chance of payoff.

Triage is one very specific response to the question "What are you trying to achieve?" The French doctors primary objective was not to create an image of compassionate caring. They were not trying to alleviate suffering at the cost of lives. They didn't care about their public image. *They were simply trying to save lives!* Having defined their objective in the clearest, most hard-headed way, they developed an efficient system to maximize that objective. The triage system would not have emerged without such a clear definition.

This concept of triage is just as valid in business operations (but without the heavy implications). Frequently managers get overwhelmed by problems that come from every direction. There is a tendency to flail away at the problems in some disorganized, unfocused way—or, worse, to deal with them as they come, regardless of their size or importance. The result is that after the day is over, we wonder where the hell the time went and what was accomplished.

One way to cut through these situations is to practice triage. Some of the problems are going to sort themselves out without too much help from you—maybe not quite as elegantly as if you did give them some time, but reasonably well. Other problems are not going to improve much despite your intervention. (For the purposes of image, you may feel you should give them *some* attention—but under the circumstances, should you really?) Finally, there is the group of issues where your attention can make a big difference. This is where your limited time and resources should go.

You may be aware of a sales and marketing concept being touted today that (unknowingly) suggests a triage approach to selling. Its practitioners point out that there are certain accounts that are going to buy from you regardless. These are long-standing accounts where your company is a perfect fit, and not too much can dislodge you. Other potential customers you can just about write off, if you are really candid with yourself. The fit just isn't there, or there is some other competing factor that makes a certain prospect a hopeless sell. Finally, there are accounts where your efforts could really make a difference: all the factors are reasonably favorable, and a little stronger sales and marketing effort could pay off handsomely. (Ironically, it has been documented that most salespeople spend an equal amount of time on each of the three groups—if not a disproportionate amount on the first group of solid customers.)

Please note that, whether it be customers or problems, I am not suggesting that you should ignore two of the three groups as a standard practice. During times when resources are most limited, triage may be the best allocation of resources.

We Screwed Up Yesterday

On about 20 occasions during the 10 years running Battery and Tire Warehouse, I played out a scenario in which I consistently achieved my objective. A salesman would come up to me and lament along the following lines: "We are in big trouble at Sam's 76. Joe, our driver, got into a big hassle with Sam, and I wouldn't be a bit surprised if this the last we will see of his business. Could you possibly give him a call and sort things out?"

"Sure, what's the phone number?

"Wait a minute. Let me give you the facts behind what went on."

"No, just give me the phone number."

We would then go back and forth a few times, with him wanting to fill me up with "all the facts," and with me vigorously resisting and asking for the phone number.

I'd then place a call to Sam, and my opening comment was always as follows: "Hi, Sam, this is Charlie Bodenstab, the owner of Battery and Tire Warehouse. I understand that we really screwed up over at your place yesterday. I'm calling to let you know that is not how we normally operate, and I'm sorry for any inconvenience we may have caused." I used the same message regardless of the circumstances.

I would *always* get back the following type of response: "Oh, hell, it's no big deal. Your driver Joe gets a little hot under the collar once in a while, but he really is a good guy."

This customer was supposedly going to dump us, and here he was telling me that everything was really OK. What happened? Simple: *People want to be heard, and they want to feel you care.*

On the other hand, if I had started out saying that I was calling to get to the bottom of the problem, I would have had to listen to a half-hour rendition of what the problem was.

There *was* one occasion where this approach created an odd situation. I went through the process as usual, got the phone number, and then went into my apology. The customer at the other end responded that he really wasn't sure why I was calling since things had been going along just fine. It turned out that my salesman had given me the number of the wrong account! It took me a few minutes to recover, but guess what? The call still had a pay-off, since the customer realized how we handled problems.

In all the years of my managing people, I have always found it refreshing when someone came in and candidly said, "Boy! Did I screw up this morning on such and such." As long as this isn't happening routinely, the statement says that the person is confident enough to admit the mistake, is aware of the mistake, and will no doubt take corrective action (and isn't sitting on pile of other, undisclosed screw-ups).

When confronted with a messy situation, a straight, outright, honest statement will usually work wonders. People have tremendous empathy and understanding for this response. It's the defensiveness, or the effort to transfer blame, that creates animosity and causes people to dig their heels in.

Three Acceptable Responses and One Unacceptable One

About a week before assuming ownership of BTW, I attended one of its sales and staff meetings. At the end of the meeting I commented that I really didn't have too much to say, but I was struck by something. It seemed that during the meeting a lot of apparent commitments were made to follow up on something, or to take care of something. I said that despite these voiced commitments, I had a funny feeling that no one really had any serious intention of carrying them out. (Specifically, no one had been taking any notes, and there was a certain vagueness to the atmosphere.)

After the meeting I was approached by a number of the attendees, who said, "Boy, did you hit the nail on the head. That is exactly one of the big problems around here." Interestingly, many of these same people were the very ones who had created the impression of insincerity of action.

At the next meeting I made the point that if anyone—whether a superior, peer, or subordinate—asked one of the people to do something, there were three acceptable answers and one unacceptable one.

➤ It was obviously OK to commit to do it and then come through.

➤ It was even OK to commit to do something, only to find out that later you couldn't come through, but then get back to the person who made the request with an explanation of the situation.

➤ It was also OK to say you couldn't do it and give some reasonable reason why.

➤ The one thing that was absolutely unacceptable for anyone, myself included, was to say you would do something and then not do it, while providing no feedback.

An organization cannot survive when this last alternative runs rampant. This may not seem like a very profound point, but identifying this condition and bringing it to a halt can work wonders with a disorganized or drifting business. The key is for the top executive to articulate the policy in no uncertain terms, and follow up on violations.

Once everyone in the organization can start to feel that an agreement will be acted upon, it provides a tremendous benefit for everything from morale to basic efficiency. Conversely, if you walk away from someone who has made a commitment with the feeling that it may or may not get acted upon, it has an equally large disabling effect.

The Kangaroo Jumped

When I was the COO of Kearny National, eight companies of varying sizes reported to me. Our largest subsidiary, in Atlanta, made high voltage switching equipment. The president of this company would call me periodically in a state of anguish about the latest antics of an executive who had been hired by the board of directors to promote international sales. The executive, whom will be called Norm, reported directly to the board, and was the buddy of one of the board members. In short, he was pretty much invulnerable, and there wasn't too much anyone could do about him, no matter how many problems he created for the subsidiaries.

After about the sixth call from the president that ate up an hour of my emotional capital, I asked him a question: "What if you saw a funny beast jumping across the plains, and it had a long tail and a weird pouch in the front? You asked someone what that was and he said that it was a kangaroo.

You would think, well, that is unusual, but so be it, and the next time you saw the beast you would simply note that it was another one of those kangaroos that jump." He admitted that this was most likely how he would respond—although he wondered what the hell this had to do with Norm.

I then asked him why it was, then, that when Norm acted exactly like Norm, he got all excited, as if it were the first time Norm had displayed these characteristics. Why not simply note that the kangaroo jumped?

The point is that as humans we have a very strange tendency to strongly react to people who act in a *totally predicable fashion*, even though they have acted exactly that way numerous times before. We are smart enough to not react that way when *non-humans* (kangaroos, birds, monkeys) act in a predictable way. Why can't we apply the same perspective to our fellow human beings?

This failure stems from a nasty little streak that simply wants fellow humans to conform to our own standards of behavior—regardless of how clear it is that he or she won't or can't.

This doesn't mean you must have an unlimited tolerance for any behavior. Its just that when you come upon a situation that is simply not going to change, stop expending emotional capital on a fool's errand. This is no small issue. I wish I could have back all the resources that I have seen go down the tubes where people were fretting about these situations. (Read an Ann Landers column for a few weeks and you'll see the same amount of energy being fruitlessly expended in everyday life.)

Another benefit of accepting a person's actions as a given is it allows you to focus on how to contain the potential damage that may result from those actions. As long as you rail against the ongoing repetitive behavior, you are really not focusing on corrective actions or containment.

I knew that I had proven my point with the company president when he called one day with a series of valid issues and ended the conversation with, "Oh, by the way, the kangaroo jumped."

Carefully Balance Your Risks Against the Potential Returns

I am a fervent optimist by nature—to the point where my optimism can easily cloud my judgment at critical times. To rein in this potentially

Faced with a situation where a decision on a course of action needs to be made, I create a risk-reward matrix (Figure 14.1). Across the top are two boxes indicating whether or not the environment will be accepting of a particular course of action. Down the side are listed two levels of aggressiveness in pursuing the action.

FIGURE 14.1: The Risk-Reward Matrix

	Positive Response	Negative Response
Aggressive Approach		
Less Aggressive Approach		

The next step is to fill in the boxes with a subjectively estimated number—from minus 10 to plus 10—that reflects the amount my company will gain or lose, given the combination of those two variables in that area of the matrix.

For example, the top left box assumes that I pursue an aggressive approach and it meets with the right conditions. (This is of course, the ideal situation.) I might mark this score this box with a +5.

Then I fill out the remaining boxes with their scores. A less aggressive approach encountering a positive situation may still be a +3. A less aggressive approach encountering a negative situation might be a zero.

The last box is the most interesting one—and the heart of the issue. If I assume an aggressive approach and encounter a negative situation, what are the likely consequences? I have often found myself admitting that this score could easily be a minus 10, which is rather frightening. This specific combination of events tends to have catastrophic results. See Figure 14.2 for the sample matrix.

FIGURE 14.2: Sample of a Risk-Reward Matrix

	Positive Response	Negative Response
Aggressive Approach	+5	-10
Less Aggressive Approach	+3	0

What becomes apparent from this seat-of-the-pants risk-benefit analysis is that an aggressive approach in this particular example is neither wise nor reasonable. I could be risking the company's existence for an outcome that is simply not worth it. A less aggressive movement *in the same direction*, however, would seem to be wise, reasonable, and low risk.

I have encountered this situation many times. In one case I was an adviser for a company that had a very interesting technical product that it was in the early stages of launching. There was an inclination on the founders part to start out with a large expensive infrastructure in anticipation of a fast take-off. The feeling was that if the structure was not in place, too many opportunities would be lost. When filling out the matrix, however, it looked a lot like the one above. So the founders stepped back, reconsidered, and decided on a more conservative, low-key approach. It was agreed we could miss some opportunities as a result, but not to the point of being out of the running, or even hurting the chances of becoming quite successful (the +3 rating). If we acted aggressively however, and the conditions were not initially receptive, then we were talking doomsville. (As it turned out, the old adage that everything takes twice as long and comes in at half the pace proved true, and the more low-key, prudent approach saved our hides.)

None of this discussion should be construed to mean that you should be averse to risk taking. There are times when the matrix comes out radically different than in the example above, and aggressiveness is the only wise course.

This concept is applicable to your personal life objectives as well. Specifically, too often you risk a lifestyle (one that has become fundamental to who you are) for a chance at one that you really don't need (at best it may yield a level of added income that would not substantially change the way you live).

I had a particularly frightening reminder of this issue not too long ago. I was involved with a very rapidly-growing software company that was chronically in need of cash even though it was posting reasonable profits. In the process of lining up a very significant bank credit line, I agreed to become one of the loan guarantors. The loan had a provision of cross-guarantees—i.e. each party could be held responsible for any or all the loan. Since I had the deepest pockets of the group, this meant I was potentially on the hook for the entire amount—which would have wiped me out!

I was rather subtly drawn into this situation, so the full implications did not hit me straight off. After all, the company was profitable, it had a great product, and I felt that I had sufficient control over where the company was going to protect my interests. Before long, however, I realized that I had violated one of my cardinal rules: *Never jeopardize your existing lifestyle for a lifestyle that you really do not need.* What in God's name was I doing jeopardizing my very comfortable existence for incremental income that was not that important to me?

It so happened, despite all the positive aspects of the company, it did get into deep trouble. The company grew too fast, it was becoming mismanaged, and I had been methodically frozen out of the key decision-making process. Fortunately, I managed to get the entire line of credit refinanced through a venture capital group, which allowed me to withdraw from the guarantees. Close call!

On the surface, it sounds as though this principle would stifle aggressive investment and the entrepreneur, spirited attitude of "going for the gold!"

Maybe so. For entrepreneurs there is a tremendous tendency to risk in the opposite direction however, and my advice is just an attempt to bring things back to some middle ground.

Note, that I am not suggesting you do not take risks for a lifestyle that you do want. There comes a point in life, however, where you are enjoying life as it should be, and another layer of wealth isn't really going to change that lifestyle. When that is the case, what is the point of the risk?

You could argue that unless risks of this nature were taken, where would this country be? It is the this kind of courageous risk taking that has lead to great companies. Besides, look at all the success stories. They took the risks and look at the rewards.

All of this is true, but I am offering advice that is intended to relate to your personal well being, not the well being of society as a whole. It is best for society if more and more people took big risks, since eventually some pay off and society as whole gains. The trouble is that the road is strewn with the corpses of the ones that did not make it.

In summary, just do a reality check when you are ready to embark on a risky situation. How big is the risk in proportion to your net worth? Will it improve your lifestyle in a way that has meaning to you and your family? What are your motivations behind this action?

In a sense, you are back to that most basic question: "What am I trying to achieve?" Once you understand what you are trying to achieve, and have weighed the risk against the return and the consequences of each—then go for it if it all adds up. On the other hand, if it doesn't add up favorably, step back and look at the alternatives more closely.

Looking Up the Event Chain

Read about a dozen very successful entrepreneurs, and the sequence of decisions they made that resulted in their eventual impressive success. The thought follows; "Boy, that all makes sense: I should be doing that." What you *don't* see, and the press certainly doesn't write about, are the *other* hundred people who started ventures at the same time as the few successful ones. These other people made many of the same types of decisions, using much the same logic—but their companies are no longer around. When you focus only on the successful people, you are looking at the end process of a series of events in an event chain, and seeing only the final links of the chain.

This phenomena is beautifully illustrated in one of the great congames of all times. It goes as follows: you receive a letter accurately predicting a key event in the future, such as a boxing match. A week later you get another letter accurately predicting another event, such as an election run-off. This process goes on for another three or four weeks. You receive six letters, and six predictions, and each time the letter is dead-on. Finally a letter arrives that states, "I hope you have been able to make good financial use of my predictions, and I hope that you also realize the predictive powers that I possess. I would like to participate in your good fortune, and if you send me $500 in the return mail I will continue to send you my accurate predictions."

Fantastic! How can you go wrong? This fellow has hit six consecutive predictions on the nose. (Statistically, the probability of hitting six evenly possible predictions by chance is only about 1.5 percent.)

The fact is the schemer started out with 5,000 letters, of which half predicted the outcome of the boxing match one way, the other half the other way. When the actual event occurred, he ignored the people who received inaccurate predictions, and sent the remainder letters about the upcoming election. Half of these made one prediction, the other half the opposite. The schemer then repeated the process over six events. Eventually, he had about 75 recipients where he had a 100 percent perfect record.

Notice how different the process appears, depending on which end of the event chain you are observing. It is clear now what has been going on. Because you have been looking *up* the event chain, you saw what appeared to be an amazing ability to predict future outcomes. But if you look *down* the event chain from the other end, and observe the actual sequence of events that lead to the final results, you see that it is I nothing more than a carefully-planned hoax.

This same phenomenon takes place constantly in the business world, although not necessarily due to premeditated fraud. (On the other hand, what else are the pyramid schemes that arise periodically, and that always seem to get their share of takers?)

It is very easy to become enamored of a situation that appears to be the outgrowth of a particular strategy, when in fact it may be just the surviving event of a number of debacles.

The point, therefore, is to have a healthy awareness of this phenomenon, and guard against being lured into a fatal decision by the illusion of a prior success story. Step back and ask yourself, " what is the actual sequence of events that preceded the final outcome?" Then ask, by way of follow-up, "what branches of the event chain need to be checked out first in order to make the right decision?"

Sick Plants

When I assumed the responsibility for running the automotive battery division of Gould in the mid-1970s, we had 11 plants throughout the country. A third of the plants were doing very well, another third were doing relatively OK, and a third were having problems. What was surprising, however, was the prior management had treated all the plants as if they were in the same state of health. They were all jerked around with volume changes, product changes, new programs, you name it. In fact, the plant in St. Paul, which was very close to headquarters, had some of the biggest problems. Because of its close proximity to headquarters, it was the most heavily burdened with special requirements. A lot of the more advanced engineering work was being piloted there, and the plant suffered innumerable interruptions by visitors of all sorts.

This St. Paul plant, and two others, were sick and needed appropriate treatment. I asked my VP of operations, "If you were the coach of a basketball team and one of your players was sick with the flu, would you sign him up for a key position?" He said that obviously he wouldn't. In fact, he said that he would send the player to bed and make sure that he got plenty of tender loving care.

I said, "Great. That is what we are going to do with our three sick plants. They are going to be stabilized and get plenty of tender loving care to put them on the road to health." Their production levels were frozen and interruptions and visitors were restricted. All pilot development work was pulled and the remaining plants were required to take up the slack in all these areas.

The research director, who was a formidable man with great industry credentials, blew his stack. He was upset that his engineers were now going to have to travel to other plants for development work. He also couldn't take visitors over to the St. Paul plant on a moment's notice anymore. And so on and on.

Getting this plant in shape had profit implications that were so profound that it made all these lamentations trivial. It was just a case of prerogatives. We simply had to get our priorities in order.

Treating an organization or manufacturing operation that is having serious problems as if it were a sick patient needing appropriate ministrations can make a big difference in bringing it around to health. It has worked over and over.

All too often management further burdens operations that were in a sad state, routinely failing to recognize, let alone address, their sick status. Yet it is by classifying an operation as sick, and stabilizing the conditions around it, that the stage for recovery is set.

Summary

> **Data** is measurements and observations. **Information** results when data is processed to extract items that focus attention and trigger action. **Knowledge** is a body of organized information that enables us to generalize and predict. **Wisdom** is understanding what a body of knowledge means, how it fits into a larger context, and how to act wisely on it.

> Don't keep solving recurring problems that emanate from the same source. Instead, turn off the faucet: find out what is flawed in the first place and correct the problem at its source.

> One of the best questions you can ask before you act—and one of the best sanity checks in business—is "What are you trying to achieve?"

> The principle of triage applies as much in business as it does on a battlefield where it was first developed. If you are in a desperate time crunch, don't spend much time on the problems that will reasonably sort themselves out without your involvement—or on those that you really can't do much about. Instead, focus your energy and your limited time where your attention can make a difference.

> Be willing to admit openly when you or your organization has screwed up. This simple acknowledgment usually works wonders with a messy situation, creating empathy instead of animosity.

> An organization cannot survive when its people disregard their own promises to take action. While it is acceptable to refuse a particular task for reasonable cause—or even to fail to fulfill a commitment *if* the person to whom the commitment was made is given and explanation—it is *not* acceptable for anyone (including the CEO) to agree to do something, not do it, and provide no feedback

or explanation. The key here is for the top executive to clearly set such a policy, then follow up on any violations.

➤ Recognize that there will be times when you will have to work with people who act in ways that you feel are unreasonable. The situation will be a given and will not change. Just as a kangaroo will consistently act like a kangaroo, don't react every time the person repeats his or her predictable performance. It wastes time and emotional capital.

➤ As an aid in making important decisions, create a risk-reward matrix, as described on page 117. Using this matrix, you can carefully balance your risks against potential return. Pay special attention to the consequences for your organization (and yourself) should you commit to an aggressive approach, then encounter a negative situation. Bottom line: never risk your lifestyle for one that offers little extra in quality of life.

➤ Be aware of which end of an event chain you are looking at. Be leery of successful outcomes that may be in truth the random result of many other similar events that ended in failure—but were never reported or publicized.

➤ If a plant, unit, or division is doing badly, recognize that it is sick, and treat it as you would a sick human. Stabilize its environment, treat it with loving care, and create the conditions that will bring it back to health.

About the Author

Charles J. Bodenstab is an author, consultant, and seminar leader whose articles on management and information technology have appeared regularly in *Inc.* magazine. His first book, *A New Era in Inventory Management* (Hilta Press, 1993) has become a definitive work in the field, and is now in its second printing.

As a consultant, Mr. Bodenstab has worked with clients such as AT&T, IBM, 3M, and many other large and mid-sized corporations. He has previously served as Chief Operating Officer of Kearney National, Vice President and General Manager for Gould, Inc., Group Vice President for General Cable, and Manager for Operations Research for U.S. Steel.

Mr. Bodenstab has led hundreds of seminars on running businesses more effectively. These seminars have been sponsored by organizations that include IBM, Unisys, Hewlett-Packard, Price Waterhouse, Data General, and dozens of other large and mid-sized corporations.

In both his books and magazine articles, Mr. Bodenstab focuses on providing extremely practical information in a highly readable and accessible form.

He recently moved to San Juan Island, Washington and travels frequently throughout North America to offer seminars and consulting services.

About Charles J. Bodenstab's First Book

A New Era in Inventory Management (Hilta Press, 1993) develops, step by step, one of the most powerful, easy-to-use inventory replenishment systems available. In addition, it discusses some of the fundamental principles of good inventory practice and how these principles are widely violated at many businesses. Lastly, it offers techniques and ideas on how to rectify these violations rapidly and practically.

In its review of this volume, *Inventory Reduction Report* wrote, "*IRR* can't believe that a book on inventory management can be enlightening, yet entertaining. However, Charles J. Bodenstab has done it."

Stephen Baxter, Vice President of Data General Corporation, had this to say about the book: "This has to be the definitive text on how to forecast inventory correctly—an outstanding, and interesting book."

Now in its second hardcover printing, **A New Era in Inventory Management** is available for $40.00 postpaid from:

Charles J. Bodenstab
Hilta Press
5250 Hannah Island Dr.
Friday Harbor, WA 98250
612-471-7002

About MARS-95 Inventory Management System

Mr. Bodenstab has developed, in conjunction with NBDS, a PC-oriented inventory management software system that is based on the principles and concepts of his first book, **A New Era in Inventory Management**. MARS-95 easily attaches to existing software systems to bring the power and efficiency of Mr. Bodenstab's concepts to any organization.

To learn more about this system, check the MARS-95 web page at:

www.nbds.com
or call:
612-471-7002

Index

Establish A Framework For Excellence With The Successful Business Library

Fastbreaking changes in technology and the global marketplace continue to create unprecedented opportunities for businesses through the '90s. With these opportunities, however, will also come many new challenges. Today, more than ever, businesses, especially small businesses, need to excel in all areas of operation to complete and succeed in an ever-changing world.

The Successful Business Library takes you through the '90s and beyond, helping you solve the day-to-day problems you face now, and prepares you for the unexpected problems you may be facing next. You receive up-to-date and practical business solutions, which are easy to use and easy to understand. No jargon or theories, just solid, nuts-and-bolts information.

Whether you are an entrepreneur going into business for the first time or an experienced consultant trying to keep up with the latest rules and regulations, The Successful Business Library provides you with the step-by-step guidance, and action-oriented plans you need to succeed in today's world. As an added benefit, PSI Research / The Oasis Press® unconditionally guarantees your satisfaction with the purchase of any book or software program in our catalog.

Your success is our success...

At PSI Research and The Oasis Press, we take pride in helping you and 2 million other businesses grow. It's the same pride we take in watching our own business grow from two people working out of a garage in 1975 to more than 50 employees now in our award-winning building in scenic southern Oregon.

After all, your business is our business.

OASIS PRESS
BOOKS & SOFTWARE

Books that save you time & money

Entrepreneurs can learn how to find the best bank and banker for their business. Seven sections explain the basics: small banks versus large, finding the right loan, creating a perfect proposal, judging a business' worth, assessing loan documents, and restructuring.

The Small Business Insider's Guide to Bankers   *Pages: 176*
Paperback: $18.95   *ISBN: 1-55571-400-5*

Prepares a business buyer or seller for negotiations that will achieve win-win results. Shows how to determine the real worth of a business, including intangible assets such as "goodwill." Over 36 checklists and worksheets on topics such as tax impact on buyers and sellers, escrow checklists, cash flow projections, evaluating potential buyers, financing options, and many others.

Secrets of Buying and Selling a Business   *Pages: 266*
Paperback: $24.95   *ISBN: 1-55571-327-0*
Binder Edition: $39.95   *ISBN: 1-55571-326-2*

Makes understanding the economics of your business simple. Explains the basic accounting principles that relate to any business. Step-by-step instructions for generating accounting statements and interpreting them, spotting errors, and recognizing warning signs. Discusses how creditors view financial statements.

Business Owner's Guide to Accounting & Bookkeeping   *Pages: 145*
Paperback $19.95   *ISBN: 1-55571-156-1*

This book was written in plain English specifically designed to help businesses regain control of legal costs and functions. Topics include: how to find the right attorney, when to take legal work in-house, what can be controlled in litigation, the use of mediation and other consumer rights when dealing with lawyers. Save up to 75% of your company's legal expenses and learn ways to keep problems from becoming legal disputes.

Legal Expense Defense   *Pages: 336*
Paperback: $19.95   *ISBN: 1-55571-348-3*
Binder Edition: $39.95   *ISBN: 1-55571-349-1*

Call toll free to order 1-800-228-2275 PSI Research 300 North Valley Drive, Grants Pass, OR 97526 FAX 541-476-1479

THE OASIS PRESS® ORDER FORM

Call, Mail, Email, or Fax Your Order to: PSI Research, 300 North Valley Drive, Grants Pass, OR 97526 USA
Email: psi2@magick.net   Website: http://www.psi-research.com
Order Phone USA & Canada: +1 800 228-2275   Inquiries & International Orders: +1 541 479-9464   Fax: +1 541 476-1479

TITLE	✔ BINDER	✔ PAPERBACK	QUANTITY	COST
Bottom Line Basics	❏ $39.95	❏ $19.95		
The Business Environmental Handbook	❏ $39.95	❏ $19.95		
Business Owner's Guide to Accounting & Bookkeeping		❏ $19.95		
Buyer's Guide to Business Insurance	❏ $39.95	❏ $19.95		
Collection Techniques for a Small Business	❏ $39.95	❏ $19.95		
A Company Policy and Personnel Workbook	❏ $49.95	❏ $29.95		
Company Relocation Handbook	❏ $39.95	❏ $19.95		
CompControl: The Secrets of Reducing Worker's Compensation Costs	❏ $39.95	❏ $19.95		
Complete Book of Business Forms		❏ $19.95		
Customer Engineering: Cutting Edge Selling Strategies	❏ $39.95	❏ $19.95		
Develop & Market Your Creative Ideas		❏ $15.95		
Doing Business in Russia		❏ $19.95		
Draw The Line: A Sexual Harassment Free Workplace		❏ $17.95		
The Essential Corporation Handbook		❏ $21.95		
The Essential Limited Liability Company Handbook	❏ $39.95	❏ $21.95		
Export Now: A Guide for Small Business	❏ $39.95	❏ $24.95		
Financial Management Techniques for Small Business	❏ $39.95	❏ $19.95		
Financing Your Small Business		❏ $19.95		
Franchise Bible: How to Buy a Franchise or Franchise Your Own Business	❏ $39.95	❏ $24.95		
Friendship Marketing: Growing Your Business by Cultivating Strategic Relationships		❏ $18.95		
Home Business Made Easy		❏ $19.95		
Incorporating Without A Lawyer (Available for 32 states) SPECIFY STATE:		❏ $24.95		
Joysticks, Blinking Lights and Thrills		❏ $18.95		
The Insider's Guide to Small Business Loans	❏ $29.95	❏ $19.95		
InstaCorp – Incorporate In Any State (Book & Software)		❏ $29.95		
Keeping Score: An Inside Look at Sports Marketing		❏ $18.95		
Know Your Market: How to Do Low-Cost Market Research	❏ $39.95	❏ $19.95		
Legal Expense Defense: How to Control Your Business' Legal Costs and Problems	❏ $39.95	❏ $19.95		
Location, Location, Location: How to Select the Best Site for Your Business		❏ $19.95		
Mail Order Legal Guide	❏ $45.00	❏ $29.95		
Managing People: A Practical Guide		❏ $21.95		
Marketing Mastery: Your Seven Step Guide to Success	❏ $39.95	❏ $19.95		
The Money Connection: Where and How to Apply for Business Loans and Venture Capital	❏ $39.95	❏ $24.95		
People Investment	❏ $39.95	❏ $19.95		
Power Marketing for Small Business	❏ $39.95	❏ $19.95		
Profit Power: 101 Pointers to Give Your Business a Competitive Edge		❏ $19.95		
Proposal Development: How to Respond and Win the Bid	❏ $39.95	❏ $21.95		
Raising Capital	❏ $39.95	❏ $19.95		
Retail in Detail: How to Start and Manage a Small Retail Business		❏ $15.95		
Secrets to Buying and Selling a Business		❏ $24.95		
Secure Your Future: Financial Planning at Any Age	❏ $39.95	❏ $19.95		
The Small Business Insider's Guide to Bankers		❏ $18.95		
Start Your Business (Available as a book and disk package – see back)		❏ $ 9.95 (without disk)		
Starting and Operating a Business in...series Includes FEDERAL section PLUS ONE STATE section ❏ $34.95		❏ $27.95		
PLEASE SPECIFY WHICH STATE(S) YOU WANT:				
STATE SECTION ONLY (BINDER NOT INCLUDED) SPECIFY STATE(S):	❏ $8.95			
FEDERAL SECTION ONLY (BINDER NOT INCLUDED)	❏ $12.95			
U.S. EDITION (FEDERAL SECTION – 50 STATES AND WASHINGTON DC IN 11-BINDER SET)	❏ $295.95			
Successful Business Plan: Secrets & Strategies	❏ $49.95	❏ $27.95		
Successful Network Marketing for The 21st Century		❏ $15.95		
Surviving and Prospering in a Business Partnership	❏ $39.95	❏ $19.95		
TargetSmart! Database Marketing for the Small Business		❏ $19.95		
Top Tax Saving Ideas for Today's Small Business		❏ $16.95		
Which Business? Help in Selecting Your New Venture		❏ $18.95		
Write Your Own Business Contracts	❏ $39.95	❏ $24.95		

BOOK SUB-TOTAL (FIGURE YOUR TOTAL AMOUNT ON THE OTHER SIDE)

OASIS SOFTWARE Please check Macintosh or 3-1/2" Disk for IBM-PC & Compatibles

TITLE	3-1/2" IBM Disk	Mac	Price	QUANTITY	COST
California Corporation Formation Package ASCII Software	☐	☐	$ 39.95		
Company Policy & Personnel Software Text Files	☐	☐	$ 49.95		
Financial Management Techniques (Full Standalone)	☐		$ 99.95		
Financial Templates	☐	☐	$ 69.95		
The Insurance Assistant Software (Full Standalone)	☐		$ 29.95		
Start A Business (Full Standalone)	☐		$ 49.95		
Start Your Business (Software for Windows™)	☐		$ 19.95		
Successful Business Plan (Software for Windows™)	☐		$ 99.95		
Successful Business Plan Templates	☐	☐	$ 69.95		
The Survey Genie - Customer Edition (Full Standalone)	☐		$149.95		
The Survey Genie - Employee Edition (Full Standalone)	☐		$149.95		
SOFTWARE SUB-TOTAL					

BOOK & DISK PACKAGES Please check whether you use Macintosh or 3-1/2" Disk for IBM-PC & Compatibles

TITLE	IBM-PC	Mac	BINDER	PAPERBACK	QUANTITY	COST
The Buyer's Guide to Business Insurance w/ Insurance Assistant	☐		☐$ 59.95	☐$ 39.95		
California Corporation Formation Binder Book & ASCII Software	☐	☐	☐$ 69.95	☐$ 59.95		
Company Policy & Personnel Book & Software Text Files	☐	☐	☐$ 89.95	☐$ 69.95		
Financial Management Techniques Book & Software	☐		☐$129.95	☐$ 119.95		
Start Your Business Paperback & Software (Software for Windows™)	☐			☐$ 24.95		
Successful Business Plan Book & Software for Windows™	☐		☐$125.95	☐ $109.95		
Successful Business Plan Book & Software Templates	☐	☐	☐$109.95	☐$ 89.95		
BOOK & DISK PACKAGE TOTAL						

AUDIO CASSETTES

TITLE	Price	QUANTITY	COST
Power Marketing Tools For Small Business	☐ $ 49.95		
The Secrets To Buying & Selling A Business	☐ $ 49.95		
AUDIO CASSETTE SUB-TOTAL			

OASIS SUCCESS KITS Call for more information about these products

TITLE	Price	QUANTITY	COST
Start-Up Success Kit	☐ $ 39.95		
Business At Home Success Kit	☐ $ 39.95		
Financial Management Success Kit	☐ $ 44.95		
Personnel Success Kit	☐ $ 44.95		
Marketing Success Kit	☐ $ 44.95		
OASIS SUCCESS KITS TOTAL			

COMBINED SUB-TOTAL (FROM THIS SIDE)

SOLD TO: *Please give street address*

NAME:

Title:

Company:

Street Address:

City/State/Zip:

Daytime Phone: Email:

SHIP TO: *If different than above, please give alternate street address*

NAME:

Title:

Company:

Street Address:

City/State/Zip:

Daytime Phone:

YOUR GRAND TOTAL

SUB-TOTALS (from other side)	$
SUB-TOTALS (from this side)	$
SHIPPING (see chart below)	$
TOTAL ORDER	$

If your purchase is:	Shipping costs within the USA:
$0 - $25	$5.00
$25.01 - $50	$6.00
$50.01 - $100	$7.00
$100.01 - $175	$9.00
$175.01 - $250	$13.00
$250.01 - $500	$18.00
$500.01+	4% of total merchandise

PAYMENT INFORMATION: *Rush service is available, call for details.*
International and Canadian Orders: Please call for quote on shipping.

☐ CHECK Enclosed payable to PSI Research   Charge: ☐ VISA   ☐ MASTERCARD   ☐ AMEX   ☐ DISCOVER

Card Number: Expires:

Signature: Name On Card:

Insta06/97

Call toll free to order 1-800-228-2275 PSI Research 300 North Valley Drive, Grants Pass, OR 97526 FAX 541-476-1479

Use this form to register for an advance notification of updates, new books and software releases, plus special customer discounts!

Please answer these questions to let us know how our products are working for you, and what we could do to serve you better.

Information Breakthrough

This book format is:
- ☐ Binder book
- ☐ Paperback book
- ☐ Book/Software Combination
- ☐ Software only

Rate this product's overall quality of information:
- ☐ Excellent
- ☐ Good
- ☐ Fair
- ☐ Poor

Rate the quality of printed materials:
- ☐ Excellent
- ☐ Good
- ☐ Fair
- ☐ Poor

Rate the format:
- ☐ Excellent
- ☐ Good
- ☐ Fair
- ☐ Poor

Did the product provide what you needed?
- ☐ Yes ☐ No

If not, what should be added?
_____
_____
_____

This product is:
- ☐ Clear and easy to follow
- ☐ Too complicated
- ☐ Too elementary

Were the worksheets (if any) easy to use?
- ☐ Yes ☐ No ☐ N/A

Should we include?
- ☐ More worksheets
- ☐ Fewer worksheets
- ☐ No worksheets

How do you feel about the price?
- ☐ Lower than expected
- ☐ About right
- ☐ Too expensive

How many employees are in your company?
- ☐ Under 10 employees
- ☐ 10 - 50 employees
- ☐ 51 - 99 employees
- ☐ 100 - 250 employees
- ☐ Over 250 employees

How many people in the city your company is in?
- ☐ 50,000 - 100,000
- ☐ 100,000 - 500,000
- ☐ 500,000 - 1,000,000
- ☐ Over 1,000,000
- ☐ Rural (Under 50,000)

What is your type of business?
- ☐ Retail
- ☐ Service
- ☐ Government
- ☐ Manufacturing
- ☐ Distributor
- ☐ Education

What types of products or services do you sell?
_____
_____
_____

What is your position in the company?
(please check one)
- ☐ Owner
- ☐ Administrative
- ☐ Sales/Marketing
- ☐ Finance
- ☐ Human Resources
- ☐ Production
- ☐ Operations
- ☐ Computer/MIS

How did you learn about this product?
- ☐ Recommended by a friend
- ☐ Used in a seminar or class
- ☐ Have used other PSI products
- ☐ Received a mailing
- ☐ Saw in bookstore
- ☐ Saw in library
- ☐ Saw review in:
  - ☐ Newspaper
  - ☐ Magazine
  - ☐ Radio/TV

Where did you buy this product?
- ☐ Catalog
- ☐ Bookstore
- ☐ Office supply
- ☐ Consultant

Would you purchase other business tools from us?
- ☐ Yes ☐ No

If so, which products interest you?
- ☐ EXECARDS™ Communications Tools
- ☐ Books for business
- ☐ Software

Would you recommend this product to a friend?
- ☐ Yes ☐ No

Do you use a personal computer?
- ☐ Yes ☐ No

If yes, which?
- ☐ Macintosh
- ☐ IBM/compatible

Check all the ways you use computers?
- ☐ Word processing
- ☐ Accounting
- ☐ Spreadsheet
- ☐ Inventory
- ☐ Order processing
- ☐ Design/Graphics
- ☐ General Data Base
- ☐ Customer Information
- ☐ Scheduling

May we call you to follow up on your comments?
- ☐ Yes ☐ No

May we add your name to our mailing list? ☐ Yes ☐ No

If you'd like us to send associates or friends a catalog, just list names and addresses on back.

Is there anything we should do to improve our products?
_____

Just fill in your name and address here, fold (see back) and mail.

Name _____

Title _____

Company _____

Phone _____

Address _____

City/State/Zip _____

Email Address (Home) _____ (Business) _____

08/97

If you have friends or associates who might appreciate receiving our catalogs, please list here. Thanks!

Name_____   Name_____

Title_____   Title_____

Company_____   Company_____

Phone_____   Phone_____

Address_____   Address_____

Address_____   Address_____

FOLD HERE FIRST

‖‖‖

BUSINESS REPLY MAIL

FIRST CLASS MAIL PERMIT NO. 002 MERLIN, OREGON

POSTAGE WILL BE PAID BY ADDRESSEE

PSI Research
PO BOX 1414
Merlin OR 97532-9900

FOLD HERE SECOND, THEN TAPE TOGETHER

✂
Please cut
along this
vertical line,
fold twice,
tape together
and mail.